# Advance Praise for
# *Life After Kevin*

*Life After Kevin is heartfelt, fascinating, well written, and easy to read. You will cry with her, not only because her story is heartbreaking, but because you see yourself in her words. She's beautifully balanced the retelling of her own experiences while simultaneously inviting the reader to explore two topics not usually discussed in grief, the effects of stigma over how a person dies and how comfort can often be found in what we cannot explain with logic, such as signs from across the veil or the unconditional love from our dogs. You will love this book. Susan's writing style is direct and honest and in the back of the book she's included questions to help readers gain insight into their own experiences with grief, stigma, signs, and the relationship they have with the dogs in their lives. Read this book and learn from it. I did.*

—Jonathan C. Chase, AKC Licensed Judge

*Susan captures in intimate detail, the life, death, and precise after life communication from her beloved son, Kevin. This beautiful and important book will help guide those lost in grief to a place of peace. Her courageous journey inspires readers to know they can make it through the fire. It is a MUST read.*

—Tina Powers, Medium and
Author of *Reporting for the Other Side*

*Susan Lynch's new book,* Life After Kevin: A Mother's Search for Peace and the Golden Retrievers that Led the Way, *is a poignant memoir about the tragic passing of her beautiful son, Kevin. Through this book, Susan shows how the tenderhearted goldens that she trains helped her move forward and heal. Susan also explores an essential topic in the book with grace and compassion: the stigma and silence attached to a child's transition by overdose. It is a joy to read about the interaction they share even five years after Kevin's transition. Our kids in spirit are not gone. They are still right here and walk beside us, holding our hands and leading us towards healing. Thank you, Susan and Kevin, for this uplifting book that proves that love never dies.*

—Elizabeth Boisson, President, and
Co-Founder of Helping Parents Heal

*I thoroughly enjoyed reading* Life After Kevin: A Mother's Search for Peace and the Golden Retrievers that Led the Way. *I know it will be helpful to many who find themselves on a grief journey. Susan is a wonderful storyteller and shares her heart with her readers. Anyone who has lived through the passing of a child/ children will understand the experiences and emotions Susan describes. The death of a loved one changes our life forever, and*

*Susan offers hope through her story. Realizing that we continue a relationship beyond the veil changes everything, and Susan shares her transformation and her new relationship with Kevin.*

—Irene Vouvalides, Vice President,
Helping Parents Heal

*I absolutely loved Susan's book. I enjoyed hearing about the wonderful signs she receives from her son. This book will help so many who struggle through a number of different emotions following the passing of a child. I also love how Susan chooses to focus on helping others in many ways, including certifying her sweet golden retriever as a therapy dog who not only helps her in her grief but helps others as well. I highly recommend this book.*

—Carol Allen, Author and Director,
Helping Parents Heal

*Much like a white-water rafting trip Susan takes with her family early on in this book, her story about love, loss, grief, and healing takes us on a surprising ride. From the opening passages, Susan grabs our attention, hangs on to it tightly, and never lets go, taking us along on an emotional, complicated, powerful, and ultimately uplifting journey following the death of her son, Kevin. Susan's journey and the steps along the way will resonate with anyone who has grieved the loss of a loved one, whether human or canine, or with anyone who seeks messages from those they have lost. There's something here for everyone, but most will certainly leave with hope and just maybe with their eyes and minds open a little wider.*

—Sabrina

*If you're looking for a soul-bearing emotional read, you'll have a difficult time putting this book down. Susan's skillfully written true story drew me in and held onto my heart. It's an incredibly brave examination of her struggle to come to terms with her innermost fears surrounding her son's death. Her hopeful and insightful search for meaning after loss will have you crying, laughing, and looking inward.*

—Patricia

*Having lost an adult child myself to an accidental overdose, I know only too well the struggle and determination needed to process the loss and return to some semblance of "normal." I want my friends and family to read* Life After Kevin—*not that I want sympathy but rather acknowledgement. I want them to "get me." Susan's book is honest and sincere. It invokes questions about grief, healing, spirituality, and sadly, the stigma over the cause of death.*

—Deb

*I loved this book! I wasn't ready for it to end. I cried and laughed for two days. I couldn't put it down. What I loved the most was how Susan shared every little detail of certain memories with her son, which made him feel alive on the page but also reminded me of how I remember my dad and brother who have both passed on. Equally as important, in reading Susan's book, I now understand more of my mother's grief. I would recommend this book to anyone who has experienced grief but especially to those who have had a loved one die from overdose.*

–Amy

*I thoroughly enjoyed Susan Lynch's book* Life After Kevin. *This book brought both tears and laughter along with the reality of pain followed by hope.*

–Lynn

*Susan has written so courageously about her journey after the tragic loss of her son, Kevin. The details were so beautifully woven in with the love of her dogs and how she learned to accept and live on. This book will help others who have gone through this as well!*

–Katie

Life After Kevin *is an incredibly powerful, heartfelt, and spiritual memoir. Lynch's love for her son and the golden retrievers that led her way to peace shines through every page. Anyone who has lost a loved one will find some part of this book that resonates with them. After reading Lynch's beautiful tribute to her son, I was left feeling assured that no matter what happens, we can find a connection to our loved ones even after they have passed on.*

–Paula

*Susan's book outlines a remarkable journey. It's raw in its honesty and occasionally brought a tear to my eye. I think it gives the reader a perspective, and not preaching, on how she handled grief with all its ups and downs. I think this book will be a very good resource for people in a similar situation. In my view, very well done.*

–Larry

Life After Kevin *is a moving and tender account of the author's loss of her son, Kevin, and the golden retrievers, Tripp and Manny, who helped her survive. Susan opens the door to her heart and shares with her readers all the heartbreaking emotions that a bereaved parent goes through and more. I highly recommend this beautiful and touching story of grief; heartache; and finally, a celebration of sorts as Susan and Kevin find a way to connect. Definitely a must read.*

–Marta

*Such a hard, funny, sad, insightful read that gave me a better understanding of grief. It is a process that needs to be worked on by allowing yourself the time and attention because it's not going to happen overnight. This book will help a lot of people with their loss.*

–Gail

# Life After Kevin

# Life After Kevin

A Mother's Search for Peace
and the Golden Retrievers
that Led the Way

*A Memoir*

## SUSAN LYNCH

BMcTALKS Press
4980 South Alma School Road
Suite 2-493
Chandler, Arizona 85248

FIRST EDITION

Library of Congress Control Number: 2022905007

Paperback: 978-1-953315-21-2
eBook: 978-1-953315-22-9

Cover and interior design by Medlar Publishing Solutions Pvt Ltd., India.
Cover photo: Jackie Matthews
Back cover photo of author: Karen Tassinari

Printed in the United States of America.

*To my husband Tom, my most treasured yes.*
*You have my heart, always.*

*"... Some of you say, 'Joy is greater than sorrow,' and others say, 'Nay, sorrow is the greater.' But I say unto you, they are inseparable. Together they come, and when one sits alone with you at your board, remember that the other is asleep upon your bed ..."*

—Kahlil Gibran, "On Joy and Sorrow"

# Table of Contents

# Chapter 1

# Pura Vida

*February 2015*

You can never know at what point your memories will need to last a lifetime. For me, the last memories I have of my whole family together are from February of 2015, vacationing in Costa Rica. The vacation was to commemorate my in-laws' fiftieth wedding anniversary and included their four sons and their respective families all with much younger children than my own—seventeen of us in total.

My husband, Tom, and I were at a different point in our lives and had recently become empty nesters. Matthew, our oldest, had been in Canada since college and was living in Montreal. Kevin, our youngest, who had been California Dreamin' for a few years, had just moved from our home in New Hampshire to California. This was the first vacation the four of us had taken together in years, but I never would have imagined it would be our last.

In order to manage the activities for seventeen people, we had an agenda with booked excursions. Our "free days" with no excursions consisted of either the beach or hanging out at the villa. Costa Rica is all about having adventures, which is unfortunate for me because I am a bit of a chicken. I am usually the one watching the action and silently worrying about safety.

Earlier in the week my sister-in-law had been stung by a jellyfish, and Tom and I had been caught in a mild riptide. These mishaps were just from casually swimming in the ocean, so to do something *risky* when out of the country is just not in my wheelhouse. Needless to say, hanging out at the villa wasn't the worst thing.

It was 6,000 square feet of luxury that included 7 bedrooms, 7.5 baths, an infinity edge pool, pool house, and 3,000 square feet of deck terraces that allowed close up viewing of the lush jungle. Three-toed sloths, howler and Caspian monkeys, and yellow-throated toucans were common sights and sounds from the deck. Howler monkeys are about the size of a chimpanzee but are among the loudest animals on earth. I can attest to this as they would gather in the trees just outside of our bedroom at dawn. The sound was like a combination of a gorilla roaring and an air raid siren. Every morning I would pad down to the kitchen to grab a cup of the amazing Costa Rican coffee, head out to the deck that was overlooking the Pacific Ocean, and watch for monkeys traversing in the trees.

Kevin, who was determined to get as much surfing in during this trip, was often at the beach before the rest of us. Espadilla Beach was just a short drive and the closest beach to our villa. Restaurants and souvenir shops dotted the road alongside the sand. A few locals were renting jet skis and surfboards right on the beach. One of the mornings that

Kevin headed out ahead of the rest of us, he passed a vinyl banner that read "Parasailing Book Here!" Later that day, when Tom and Matthew arrived at the beach, Kevin asked them if they were interested in going parasailing. Because the three of them are the "when in Rome, do as the Romans do" types, they signed up for parasailing the next day.

Kevin loved any mode that helped him experience the freedom of the wind in his face: skateboards, bikes, diving boards, and waterskiing were all favorites. He could now add surfing, and soon parasailing, to the list. His desire for this freedom was apparent when, at a mere three years old, he asked Tom to take the training wheels off his bike and again at six when I asked him what superpower would he want if he could have just one, and he responded without hesitation. "To fly."

The morning of the parasailing adventure, Tom, Matthew, and Kevin were standing on the beach in their parasailing harnesses, nodding their heads in understanding at the Tico (what the native Costa Ricans call themselves) giving the instructions. He was very animated, crouching down toward the sand, tucking his knees to his chest. I suspected it was an attempt to bridge the language barrier.

Looking at my sons standing side by side, I was reminded how much they looked like Tom. All three were 5'10" with dirty blonde hair and light blue eyes. The Tico repeated the knee-tuck motion but more quickly this time, snapping me out of my thoughts. He pointed to the shrinking runway to indicate they were in a race with the incoming tide. The three of them laughed at something he had just said, but I was just far enough away to be out of earshot. The colored parasail behind them reminded me of the balloon Kevin had chased the summer he turned six, not long after he told me he wanted to fly.

3

It was the summer of 1996, and we had just moved to a small town in southern New Hampshire. We had attended an event called Old Home Day, which was a three-day festival to celebrate the town's 250th anniversary. It was a kid's dream with amusement rides, bands, a parade, hot air balloon rides, and a grand finale of fireworks on Saturday night.

Tom and I had taken Matthew and Kevin to the rides the day before and were planning on going back later that morning when, during breakfast, we heard a loud roar-like sound coming from outside. The four of us went into the backyard to see that the noise was coming from the propane burner filling a hot air balloon that was floating low with another balloon floating alongside it, just above the apple trees in the orchard next to our house. They were a beautiful sight with their rainbow kaleidoscope pattern against a cloudless blue sky and mountains far in the distance. I remember thinking how lucky we were to have moved to such a beautiful place.

A few minutes later, a wild-eyed Tom looked at me. "Where's Kevin?"

Captured by the glorious sights of the balloons overhead, we hadn't noticed Kevin had run off. We were searching and calling for him, but he was nowhere to be found.

*How could he be with us one minute and gone the next?*

I scrambled around the yard calling for him. Then, I saw Tom's car going up the street. He had a hunch that Kevin might have followed the balloons, and he was right.

Kevin had not only gone up the street by himself, but he also crossed Route 122, which is a two-way road with a speed limit of 45 mph. Tom found him just beyond the busy road, unscathed, and running through an open hay field, chasing after the balloons. When he finally got Kevin to stop running, he asked what the heck he was doing. Kevin was frustrated with the interruption.

"Daddy, I was gonna help them land."

Standing on the beach, I made note of the irony that, at six, he was looking to help those balloons land, and now here he was about to launch himself into the sky instead. They all laughed while they buckled their life vests, and I thought: *safety and laughing don't go hand in hand.* My risk-averse sensibilities were rearing their head. Were they paying attention? Were they going about safety protocol correctly? I didn't know one thing about parasailing; I just knew I was nervous. I kept thinking, *Relax, this is a vacation*, but my anxiety was heightening as was the temperature of the sand, which was becoming uncomfortably hot under my bare feet.

The instructor gave the boat driver a thumbs up then cupped his hands around his mouth and yelled, "Tres grandes!" This loosely translated to "In order to get these three large gringos airborne, you better floor it." In unison Tom, Kevin, and Matthew had lifted the bar to their chests, which was slightly reassuring because it meant they had understood the directions. The boat driver returned the thumbs up signal, hit the gas, and my family charged toward the water.

The bar lifted easily out of their hands, pulling the lines taught, and the colorful sail filled with the rush of air. I breathed a quick sigh of relief witnessing all three sets of knees dutifully tuck up just as they reached the water. The rainbow-colored sail ballooned with air and continued to rise. The takeoff had gone perfectly.

The colors of the sail looked spectacular against the blue sky, and I stood briefly transfixed by the beauty and freedom of the moment—the same way I had when I was lost inside the magnificence of those floating hot air balloons all those years prior. Yet, as they continued to rise, I noticed something wasn't right. Matthew and Tom were sitting parallel but Kevin, who was sitting between them, was askew, his legs swinging under Matthew's seat.

I stood on the beach watching in horror, completely helpless as the balloon continued to rise with Kevin dangling by only one attached carabiner. I couldn't bring myself to scream, but even if I could, they were too high up to hear me. Tom, always at the ready, realized what was happening and reached down for Kevin's strap. Miraculously, he was able to pull it up and clip the wayward carabiner in place, making all three orange life vests and pairs of legs even. I couldn't take my eyes off them for the duration of the ride, and my breathing didn't return to normal until after they were all safely back on the beach.

Crisis averted—this time.

* * *

Two days after the parasailing near-crisis, we were off to another adventure, and this time I participated. A whitewater rafting trip along the Savegre River had been added to the itinerary per the villa concierge's suggestion. In fairness, she described the river as category two and three rapids (which I neglected to look up), but she also said "it was calm enough to enjoy the scenery" and that her eight-year-old daughter "loved it." I chose to focus on the latter, which had me envisioning more of a scenic ride down a lazy river. *That* sounded perfect.

Every morning at the villa there was a flurry of activity with cars running and ready to depart to either the beach or an excursion. The morning scramble was in full swing for those leaving for the day with kids grabbing their bathing suits and towels from the deck railing for our white-water rafting trip. The mother in me couldn't help but ask Kevin, who was twenty-four, if he brought his water shoes. He had always had an eclectic sense when it came to clothing, and I knew full well I'd be lucky if he could come up with a mismatched pair of flip flops, never mind water shoes.

I reached for my phone that had just dinged, alerting me to a new email message. I wanted to check to see if it was from my mother who was dog-sitting my two golden retrievers, Manny and Tripp. She had been great all week about sending updates on how they were doing, knowing they were such an important part of my life—my four-legged family members. My mother, who is known to all as "Weezie," had just sent a video attachment with a short note: *I hope you are having as much fun as Manny and Tripp!*

I clicked on the link to watch Manny and Tripp back in New Hampshire having a blast, running zoomies in the snow.

Kevin walked over to me, dangling his flip flops from his finger and looking curious about what I was laughing at.

"Kev, check out the email Weezie just sent me."

I held up my phone and replayed the twenty-second video.

He laughed, took the phone from me, and tapped the screen to watch it again. Kevin adored the dogs and was chuckling, watching them zoom around in the snow at Lake Winnipesaukee where he had spent a good part of his life.

"They're having fun." He smiled and handed me the phone.

"Yes, they are," I said and slid the phone into my back pocket.

"Whasup? Are you ready to go?" I asked.

He looked up at me with that look on his face—the one that let me know he was about to plead for something. He'd had that look since he was a preschooler when he used to tap the tips of his fingers together and would only half look at me in the eye when he was about to ask for something and wasn't certain how I would respond. If I paused for even a second to think before answering his request, he'd say, "How about yes?" with a hopeful lift of his eyebrows and a small turn up of his lips into a nervous smile.

"Mom, I was thinking. You know how much I love the beach and surfing, right?"

I nodded, already understanding where this was going.

A perfect weather day for Kevin would include ninety-degree temperatures and sunshine alongside a body of water—either freshwater or salt. Born in August, Kevin's astrological sign was Leo, and as such, he was ruled by the sun. The white-water rafting was the only activity I wanted to do together as a family, and he was looking for my approval to skip it to go surfing. Kevin was an expert at enjoying the moment *except* when he believed someone was mad or disappointed in him. He definitely didn't want me affecting his surfing time, which is why he needed my approval.

He tilted his head at an angle as if he were trying to see if I had been swayed by his statement, then added, "We only have a few more days here, and I was thinking ... I was thinking I should be taking advantage of the waves and what beach time I have left."

Kevin had learned to wield his charm very early in life and always seemed to use it to his full advantage. He was a towhead with baby blue eyes and a smattering of freckles across his cheeks. When he was three, he had fallen on the last step of the front porch and scraped his nose which left a small scar. The freckles were erased by the scab, and for a few years, he referenced that part of his face as "the spot where nothing grows."

As a young adult, he hadn't lost this sense of charm, which usually gave him an unfair advantage in conversations. Nevertheless, his charm was a magnet for most people and animals who were naturally drawn to him. Except, I was his mother, and his charm only worked *some* of the time.

"Kev, I *really* want you to come with us; it won't be the same without you."

"Mom, come *onnnnn*," he said, emphasizing his frustration. "We only have three days left."

"I know Kev, but it's important to me that you come. Besides, you are going to love it; rafting is gonna be so fun," I said, raising my voice to that enthusiastic pitch, hoping it would work. "I promise you're gonna love it." Then, just for good measure, I put my hands together in prayer and whined, "Please? For me?"

We both knew this week would be the last we'd have together for a while, but I pointed it out anyway.

"These are our final days all together before the holidays, which are months away and," I quickly added, "we will probably be home around 2:00, so you should have time to go to the beach when we get back."

He considered this for a moment and relented, tipping his head back in defeat. "Ugh, okay. I'll go."

"Thanks, Kev!" I said and hugged him. "Maybe we'll see a sloth!" I added excitedly, knowing how much he loved animals.

"Mom, it's white-water rafting. Hopefully we will be going too fast to see a sloth," he said with a smirk.

His comment should have given me an inkling that this ride was going to be a little more than I was envisioning, but I was so happy he was coming I didn't consider it. Before he could change his mind, I said, "They're waiting for us. Go grab a towel!"

I've often looked back on this memory and wondered if my sixth sense was chiming in, having some higher knowing of what was to come several months later. I can't be sure, but at that moment, I had felt strongly about him coming. We just had to do this all together. All four of us needed to be on that raft.

Maybe, on some level, Kevin also knew it was important for us to be together that day as a family, but I'll never know. All I can be sure of is how strongly I felt the push to make sure he came and the relief I felt when he said he'd go.

* * *

Our guide was with the Amigos del Rio tours in Manuel Antonio. We boarded the bus taking us to Savegre River, and I noted the flora and fauna mural on the side. It didn't hide the fact it was once a school bus, and we were all chuckling about it as we took the three oversized steps aboard.

It took only fifteen minutes to get to the river, but the ride was on a neglected dirt road full of potholes from the rainy season. It was hard to have a conversation over the bus's engine and constant jostling, so I tried to distract myself by looking out the dirty window to see if I could spot a sloth. I was glad the seats in front of me were blocking my view so I didn't have to see if Kevin was pouting, regretting his decision to skip surfing. It was too bumpy for me to see much, so I sat with my eyes unfocused and let the greenery pass by.

When we arrived at the river, we were greeted by a member of the staff who had us split ourselves into three groups. My brothers-in-law and the cousins were in two rafts, and Tom, Matthew, Kevin, and I were in the third. The guides briefed each of us with safety instructions "just in case someone falls out."

I was still expecting it to be a lazy river ride even with the fact we now had an athletic looking guide standing next to our raft wearing a life jacket and wrap-around sunglasses—the kind that don't fall off easily. It still hadn't dawned on me that it might be a more aggressive ride than I had envisioned. How I missed these additional clues at the time, I don't know.

"He's coming with us?" I asked Tom.

"Yea, he helps with steering the raft in the rougher parts."

*This* was the thing that made me finally realize maybe this raft ride wasn't so lazy after all. I remember now the description of class two and three rapids and registered maybe those were actually high classes despite the low numbers. I knew then I should have Googled it.

We stood on the riverbank waiting for our guide in our matching red helmets and life vests when I asked my brother-in-law to snap a quick family picture. That photo hangs in my living room today to commemorate our last adventure. I still chuckle a little to myself when I look at it.

Matthew and Kevin claimed the front of the boat. Tom and I got in and sat behind them. Then, upon instruction, we held our paddles up in the air and collectively slapped blades in a high five before we began as was customary. I saw it as a way to solidify that we were a team and no matter how rapid or unruly the water got, we were in this together.

At first, the shallow water was calm and warm with a rocky beach on either side. The river looked to have carved out a space between the tree-lined mountains. A band of fog had settled about a third of the way up the peak. I dipped my oar in the water and gave a good pull back as we began our slow trek down the river. Our crew was not at all in sync with paddling, which (after one truly accidental splash) became deliberate, directed splashes between Matthew and Kevin.

While my sons neglected paddling to engage in revelry with each other, I was feeling Costa Rica's unofficial motto *Pura Vida*, which means "pure life" or "simple life." I was so blissfully content laughing with my family as I attempted to still paddle our rubber boat while avoiding being splashed by Kevin's and Matthew's oars. In that second, as I watched my family and listened to our laughter, I was so glad we had a commemorative picture taken before we got into the boat.

The river began to wind, making it difficult to anticipate what was ahead, which I found surprisingly exciting. The water was rougher with each new twist and turn, which made it hard to know when to paddle and when to coast.

"Left. Now!" Tom yelled.

*What does that even mean?* I thought. Since he was on the left side of the boat and I was on the right, does that mean I wait to paddle? Or does that mean we try to move the boat to the left?

I didn't give the instructions any more thought as the situation suddenly became hilarious to me. As we moved swiftly down the river, the paddling instructions started to wane as we were all overcome with laughter at how little control we had. It seemed as if we had all realized our attempts to steer the raft were fruitless, and we let the river guide us to a destination unknown.

We all shrieked as we approached a rock the size of our boat but magically avoided it. As we approached the next turn, the sound of the river and the churning white rapids had our full attention. This was no lazy river ride.

I was now crystal clear on why we were instructed on overboard protocol and briefly annoyed I didn't pay closer attention. The river was fast and thrust our boat up and down pushing the bow underwater. Muffled screams and laughter were heard over the roar of the river as water rushed over the sides of the rubber rafts. My sunglasses were spotted with water, which happened to soften the intensity of the clusters of large boulders. Our boat was moving so fast there was no way to prepare for the obstacles, never mind having any discussion over how to avoid hitting them. I was briefly concerned that the rubber boat would pop on a rock, but I was laughing too hard to pay it any real mind.

Matthew's paddle was in the air and his other hand on Kevin's knee. They were open-mouthed laughing so hard it was contagious. The rafting company's photographer was sitting right where the river gets rough, taking the pictures that prove our guide was working his butt off to keep us safe while the rest of us were truly along for the ride. In every picture, every single one of us was laughing with our paddles in the air, nowhere near the water rushing beneath us.

Finally, the river's roar quieted, depositing us into calmer waters, and we were reunited with our family in the other rafts. The buzz from the experience had everyone trying to one-up each other with near-miss stories. Our guide grabbed the pre-stashed cooler, slung it over his shoulder, and led us up the hill to a waterfall for a swim and some fruit.

The hike up to the waterfall had us hot again, and the cousins were hurrying to get their water shoes off to go swimming in the lagoon. The continuous rush of the water coming over the cliff carved a wide "U" in the giant boulder with water cascading from the edge like a shower.

I swam just beyond the shower to a cave-like area and sat on a flat rock that jetted out like a bench created by nature. Our guide climbed to the top of the boulder and stood on the edge alongside the plummeting water. He whistled to get our attention, then leapt off the ledge into the lagoon, extending an invitation for us to follow suit. The cousins hollered excitedly and scrambled out of the water and up to the ledge with Kevin trailing behind them.

The cousins assessed the height while trying to convince Kevin he should jump first. If anyone would do this, it was him and they all knew it. But Kevin did an excellent job faking hesitation by looking over the edge with feigned consideration. I've seen this stunt before. I knew he was bluffing.

Every summer since he was little, he loved to jump off a twenty-foot-high dive at the O'Tooles, my parents' neighbors on Lake Winnipesaukee. One time when he was fifteen, I had driven him to their high jump by jet ski. He had begged me to go but was slow about climbing up the ladder, which I thought was strange. Standing at the top he was biting his nails, hesitating and looking nervous. When I actually thought he might not jump, he took three running strides to the edge and did a front flip off the jump and into the lake.

When he popped up from underneath the water, my mouth was agape as he was slapping the water laughing hysterically. He knew he had not only fooled me but had shocked me with a flip. I wouldn't fall for that trick again, but his cousins didn't see it coming.

They assumed he was not going to jump and continued debating who would jump first. While they discussed, Kevin took three quick strides and launched himself off the ledge, tucking his head down into a flip and plunged into the water. *Pura Vida* may well be the Costa Rican motto, but *carpe diem* was surely Kevin's.

Three days later, we were saying our goodbyes at the Juan Santamaria International Airport in San Jose, Costa Rica. Matthew's flight home was to Montreal, Kevin's to San Francisco, and Tom and I would be heading to Boston to then drive back to New Hampshire alone—empty nesters once again. I knew Matthew would be home for a visit in a couple months, but Kevin wasn't scheduled to come home for ten more. I watched him as he walked away to his departure gate having no idea it would be the last time I would see him alive.

*Chapter 2*

# The Last Good Show

*September 27, 2015*

Seven months after our Costa Rica vacation, Manny, Tripp, and I drove from our home in New Hampshire to Wilmington, Ohio for the start of the Golden Retriever Club of America's National Specialty (often called the National). The National was right up there with Christmas and my birthday as my favorite events of the year. It is an event where I can be around hundreds of like-minded people who share my passion for golden retrievers.

They are a group of people who think it's completely normal to spend their two-week vacation driving a couple of ten-hour days across the country to go to a week-long dog show. In 2013, I drove Manny and Tripp from New Hampshire to Wichita Falls, Texas, and in 2014, I drove to Asheville, North Carolina. On any given weekend during the year, I would compete somewhere along the east coast—Maine to Maryland and also into Canada. Long road trips are a normal part of dog shows.

The National is an event where people come from all over the country to compete in a variety of venues where dog and handler teams perform to be judged on natural retrieving ability in Hunting Tests and Field Trials, their speed and dexterity in Agility, their exact execution of training in Obedience, or how their physical bodies match up to the breed standard in Conformation. Some of these venues can be miles from the main show headquarters, which is typically a large convention type hotel. The event can have 3,000 entries or more and has taken place almost every year since 1940.

Competing at the National is a unique opportunity to see dogs that live on the other side of the country and is also a *chance to be seen* performing with and against some of the best dogs in the country. Any ribbon awarded is double the size compared to the ones given out at a regular test or show. The thrill of being awarded one at a National is also double. Manny and Tripp were entered in several events, so it was my hope to be bringing home a few of these super-sized ribbons at the end of the week.

My love affair with ribbons began on a swim team at the Woburn Boys Club. I was eight years old in 1974, and although the name didn't include girls at the time, they did allow girls to swim there. My coach helped me improve my stroke so I would swim more efficiently and, thus, improve my time. I learned about success with a good coach, practice, and some talent. My efforts were recognized with a stopwatch and a polyester ribbon with the details written on the back. Stroke, length, time, and placement—all measurable.

I swam year-round competitively for years, and although it was not my passion, it did feed my competitive nature and gave me a sense of achievement. As an average student, the awards I received from competing became a replacement for the grades I wasn't getting. They gave me that *atta girl, you are really good at something* I wanted to feel. When I was eleven years old, I was awarded my first trophy and felt the intoxicating rush of pride. I would chase that feeling for the next forty years.

What I would learn along the way is that although competing filled a need in me, I was missing the feeling of connectedness. It was when I started to train my first puppy where I found that missing piece. Being able to connect and communicate with a dog nurtured the part of me that connected deeply with nature and animals. Today, when I hold a puppy in a way where I can feel his body relax, to me, it is like speaking telepathically.

Though Tripp was now three years old, I still remember the first time he tried to get my attention. He was from the first litter Manny had sired. When the litter was about six weeks old, I was watching them interact with each other when he noticed me and stopped playing with his littermates. He held my gaze, making such an effort to connect with me that I picked him up and laid him on my chest where he promptly crawled up toward my shoulder and snuggled his soft face into my neck. I had my hand on his back and could feel his body relax, making contented snuffling sounds against my ear. He spoke to me with his eyes, communicating exactly what he wanted. He had wiggled himself into my heart.

Tripp and I stood on the starting line waiting for the final series of the hunt test to begin. The judges were behind us, holding clipboards that held our scoresheets. Per usual, I was a combination of nerves, adrenaline, and concentration. The entire test was two long days outside and those multi-day events always took a toll on my body. At the end of every hunt test, I wanted a beer, a shower, and food—in that order.

Tripp had passed four previous tests toward his Master Hunter title and had done really well for most of this one. He had already retrieved six birds and had taken my hand signals, directing him to find three additional birds the judges had hidden. If he performed well on this final water series, he would have his fifth and final pass to earn his title.

This last part of the test was a double water retrieve, and he had already brought the first bird back. It was his job to remember where that last "memory" bird had landed. He was swimming toward it; but he was upwind, and it landed in a tricky spot in some grassy cover just beyond the edge of the pond on land. It was only when I saw him turn toward me with the found bird in his mouth that I was able to exhale. As I watched his blonde head glide through the water heading toward me, we locked eyes, and I filled with emotion.

We did it.

After the ribbons were handed out to the dog and handler teams that passed, I clipped the supersized orange rosette to Tripp's collar and asked a friend to snap a quick photo of us. Then, we headed back to the hotel. I especially wanted to get there quickly because I had phone calls to make to share our big news.

I walked Manny and Tripp from my truck to the potty area located on the hotel side lawn, which is marked off with rope and poop bag stations. Some vans displaying well-known kennel names and logos filled the parking lot. A few familiar faces scurried in and out of the hotel, retrieving grooming equipment from their cars. I recognized a professional handler who was talking on her phone with a freshly bathed Golden at the end of her leash. Her attention was fixed on her conversation while her dog was busy sniffing for the best spot to pee. She didn't know me, and I thought how celebrity-like she was in this dog world. *I want my dogs and myself to be that successful* I thought and kept walking.

As I passed back through the parking lot, back to the hotel, I noticed the license plates. I thought of how devoted dog people were to their breed or sport of choice. License plates from Oregon, Pennsylvania, Colorado, Ontario, Florida, and Maryland were displaying 24KK9, RETRVR, FETCH, K9BUS, AGLTY. I chuckled when I remembered my license plate had been GOLDN+ for the past twenty-five years.

I navigated the three of us into the lobby past people and their dogs and stepped into the elevator. A man in his sixties with perfectly coiffed hair in Nantucket red chinos was standing next to the button panel. He smelled clean, like shaving cream. He smiled at me. "What floor?"

"Four, please." I gave him a smile back and a nod.

Manny sniffed the man's pocket and looked up at him expecting to be petted. The man was another professional handler who was balancing a garment bag over his shoulder and holding a luggage handle in the other.

"I know you smell the cookies that *were* in that pocket," he said looking down at Manny.

Manny, who was looking up at the man's face, responded to the word "cookie" by wagging his tail.

"Sorry, buddy. They're all gone." He gave Manny an apologetic look.

The elevator dinged, and the doors opened on my floor. "Good luck this week," I said as we walked off the elevator and headed to my room.

"Thanks. You, too," he called from behind.

Tom was always my first call after any dog events, but on that day, I had the urge to call Kevin first. Kevin was my biggest cheerleader when it came to dog shows, and I knew this was going to be a good call.

I was happy to have a good reason to call him and that I was not calling to remind him of things he needed to do. The last time I called was to remind him that his Planet Fitness bill was due on the first of the month. I hated to see him have to pay another late fee and would think *If he would just set up the auto payment ...*

Maybe on some unconscious level, I knew this would be our last call and was looking for a connection between mother and son that wasn't about late fees or asthma. Maybe I intuitively knew he was available to pick up his phone, and if I had waited five minutes longer, he would be in the car with his friends; and I would have missed my chance to hear my son's voice that last time.

I swiped the key to my room and unleashed the dogs. They each laid down on their respective dog beds and started to chew on the moose antlers I had bought them. I filled their water bowl and reached for my cell phone in my back pocket, but it wasn't there.

"Did I leave it in my car?" I asked out loud as though Manny or Tripp would confirm, but they just looked at me as if to say, "I didn't touch it" and continued chewing.

*"No, no, no ..."*

I started to feel a bit uneasy knowing it was a newish iPhone and had captured precious memories—memories

I would not have wanted to lose even if nothing traumatic was about to happen.

I had bought it right before we left for Costa Rica, and I think of all the pictures I took with it. I got distracted wondering if I had backed it up when we returned from vacation. The thought of having lost my phone put me right on the edge of panic.

I grabbed my purse and dug around at the bottom.

*Where is my phone?!*

Suddenly the image of my black tote bag popped into my head.

I love it when my intuition kicks in when I need it. I'm never sure how it works, but it does and often. Conveniently, it tends to happen when I've misplaced something, and I suddenly get a clear image of the lost object. In my mind's eye, I'll get an image of my keys sitting on top of the washing machine or my wedding ring in the small dish on top of the microwave.

The tote was within arm's reach, and I anxiously rustled through it.

Voila!

I breathed a sigh of relief as I pulled out my phone.

Sitting on the side of the bed, I touched Kevin's name on my phone screen. I waited for the call to connect and figured out the time difference in California. He was three hours behind so I should be okay reaching him.

During a recent conversation, he told me the wildfire smoke had an effect on the air quality where he was living. He's had asthma since he was little and always played down how much it bothered him—mostly because I'd make him stop playing and take a rest.

Over the years, I've paid close attention to his coughing and the degree of wheezing on inhales, so I know if he's getting into trouble. Sometimes it's as subtle as how quickly he has to take a breath when talking. On a couple of occasions, I've had to take him into the ER for serious attacks.

I hear him answer. "MOTHERRRRRR!" Kevin says, knowing it's me.

He greeted me like this often, and it always sounded like he was announcing the Queen of England. He held the "R's" like trumpets were sounding, and it made me feel like a million bucks. That was his superpower.

"Hi, Kev!"

I heard a car door shut in the background, and a friend called to him. "Kevin, don't make that a long call, dude. We'll be late for the show."

His friends knew him well. Kevin was a master at the art of conversation. His entire life revolved around connecting with people. One of his friends had recently told me that she and Kevin had reconnected post-high school while in line for a bus. She had been going through a rough time, and he sat with her while she cried and told him her struggles. She said they talked for quite a while, and finally, when he felt she was okay, they got up and realized they missed their bus.

"Hang on," he called to them.

He cleared his throat, a sign his asthma was acting up. "Sup, Mom?!" I could hear the smile in his voice.

"Guess what?"

"Did Manny or Tripp win something?" His voice was hopeful and lilting.

Kevin loved to hear about my accomplishments with the dogs. He was also somewhat competitive, but he was also homesick at times. He hadn't seen "his dogs" in ten months, and hearing about them gave him that comfortable feeling of home. I had recently texted him a video of Manny eating a chunk of iceberg lettuce, and he said he watched it repeatedly, making him laugh every time.

I liked to think Kevin's love of animals came from me. My connection with animals started from a TV show and was fostered every Sunday evening while watching *Wild Kingdom* with my family. The show's host, Marlin Perkins, would take us on a thirty-minute adventure somewhere around the globe to see wild animals in their natural habitats. My favorite episodes were the ones in Africa. Nestled in my red bean bag chair, I would sit in anticipation, rooting for the lionesses who had their eyes on a zebra for their next meal, but moments later, I would feel sad when the zebra died. Marlin would comment on the circle of life, and that somehow would reconcile the conflict in my young mind.

Years later and as a parent, I could get Kevin to take a shower without complaint if I offered a small bribe of TV or a video in return. I remember one evening, after he had spent a long day of swimming and sun at Lake Winnipesaukee, I told him I'd put *The Lion King* on, one of his favorites, after he took a shower. He was old enough to shower by himself, but in his opinion, it was something grown-ups made you do for no reason—just like brushing your teeth. As a result, sometimes I would find his toothbrush wet, but his breath still smelled like chips. He knew washing his hair was part of the deal, so smelling his wet hair to confirm it had met with some shampoo needed to be done discreetly. He had sidled up next to me on the couch all clean in his favorite Ninja Turtles pajamas, and I kissed the top of his head that smelled of shampoo. This moment in time was perfect. With his damp head on my lap, we watched the animals of Africa make the pilgrimage to Pride Rock. When the giraffes came up over the hill and the song "Circle of Life" began,

I was glad he couldn't see the tears that song always stirred up for me.

I nodded even though he couldn't see me. "Yup! Tripp got his Master Hunter title!"

"Oh my God, Mom. That's awesome!"

"Thanks! Kev, you should see his ribbon. It's huge. And he's only three!" I said boastfully.

A car horn beeped. "Come on, Kev!"

"We are going to a show. I gotta go, but I'm really happy for you."

"Okay. Who are you seeing? I love you," I said, trying to keep the good vibe going a little longer.

"A Dead cover band. I love you, too."

Kevin and I shared another passion, and that was music. When he and Matthew were little, I'd put Paul Simon on, turn up the volume, and we'd dance around the living room to our favorites, "Kodachrome" and "Me and Julio Down by the Schoolyard" among others. Music was one of the few common ground subjects to discuss during the teen years, a time when parents are viewed as knowing very little. We mostly talked about classic rock bands (our mutual favorite), but in his late teens, his interest started leaning more toward the Grateful Dead of which I was not a fan.

The Grateful Dead had officially disbanded when Jerry Garcia died in 1995, but band members continued to perform in other bands such as Dead and Company, Phil Lesh and Friends, Dark Star Orchestra, and others—all of whom Kevin saw many times. The jam band culture became a passion of his, and he would go to shows almost every weekend often camping out during three-day music festivals with names like Gathering of the Vibes and Frendly Gathering. Bands such as Twiddle, Phish, and The String Cheese Incident were among some of his other favorites.

I remembered a few months prior, he was thrilled to have been able to purchase a ticket for the Grateful Dead's Fare Thee Well tour performed by the remaining survivors of the band. It was advertised as being their final tour playing altogether and consisted of only five shows, two of which were held at Levi Stadium in Santa Clara, California. Kevin had paid a handsome price for the first night's ticket and was over the moon when he was given a "miracle ticket" (free ticket) for the following night.

"Okay. I'll talk to you later." I couldn't help myself and added "Be careful."

"Ugh, okay. Bye."

*Why do I say that? He has told me a thousand times not to worry. I know it annoys him.*

But I know his history. I know he can take fun to the next level. Saying it makes me feel like I'm providing some kind of protection.

"Bye," I said.

Saying it doesn't keep him safe. That phone call was on Sunday, September 27, 2015. He would be dead six days later.

*Chapter 3*

# Homeward Bound

*October 3, 2015*

Manny and Tripp's conformation classes were that Thursday and Friday after the hunt test, but because neither dog had won their class, they would not be competing in Best of Breed Saturday morning. Since we were done with all our events, I'd decided I'd check out of the hotel Saturday morning, which would get me home a day earlier than planned. I had packed up all my grooming equipment Friday night so all I'd need to grab were the soft travel crates and last-minute toiletries.

Saturday morning, I gave the room one last scan and headed for the elevator. At 8:30 a.m., the hotel was bustling with dogs and their people. The final event of the week was conformation judging to award the Best of Breed.

I was feeling a pang of regret that I would miss the pomp and circumstance of the event, especially the ceremonial bagpipes. The golden retriever originated from Scotland and to kick off Best of Breed, they always had a few bagpipers clad in kilts, high socks, and hats while golden retriever champions and their handlers gaited around a ring the size of a basketball court.

In 2013, I had been caught off guard when I heard the bagpipes playing and watched as a professional handler showed Manny for the Best of Breed competition which had made me a little emotional. I belonged to this subculture, and I felt proud to be a part of a group that had such respect for the history and preservation of the breed. I remember standing ringside suddenly feeling underdressed in jeans and a t-shirt.

Standing in the elevator, I was attempting to keep my dogs in the corner so they wouldn't get any drool on passing garment bags containing the pressed suits soon to be worn by the handlers showing dogs. They were both taking advantage of my arms being full along with holding their leashes. I needed to remind them, especially Manny, my social butterfly, to "sit" which effectively put an end to their wanting to investigate the people and their stuff. The elevator dinged and the doors opened, letting passengers out into the lobby. Manny, Tripp, and I hung back to let all the handlers hurry out.

Stepping off the elevator, I noticed people going in and out with umbrellas. I paused to text my friend, Pat, to see if she could meet me to say goodbye. Pat and I met in the mid-1990s when I got my first golden retriever, Bailey. She had been involved in golden retrievers and dog shows since the early 1980s and has had one or more ever since. Her dad lived near me in New Hampshire and before he died, we'd always get together at his house for visits and take our dogs for walks when she was in town.

I put my phone in my pocket, slid my hood up, and headed out into the rain. I needed to let the dogs have a romp in the fenced-in area. This would be their last potty break for a few hours. While they took their bathroom break, I checked my watch. I had made a reservation for the night at the Red Roof Inn in Syracuse, New York, which would be a full day's drive, but I figured I could make it there by dark even with a few bathroom stops.

When they were done, I got them situated in the car, then squeezed our final things in. I saw Pat walking towards me in the parking lot.

*Perfect timing.*

Her club was hosting the National, so she had been running around all week. I was glad to get a chance to say goodbye. I knew we wouldn't see each other until the National the following year.

She waved, making sure I saw her, and I couldn't help but think of how much she looked like her father.

"Goodbye, my friend. See you next year," I said, hugging her. I was tired just thinking about a full day of driving. Always the planner, I asked, "By the way, where *is* the National next year?"

"Northern California," she said, stifling a yawn.

*Too far,* I think. "I'll probably skip that one and plan for 2017 when it's back on the east coast."

"Oh yea. I heard it's going to be in Maryland in 2017," she replied.

I bent again to hug her small frame, "You guys did such a great job hosting this year, everything was spectacular."

"Thanks. I think it went well, too. Safe travels and say 'hello' to Tom for me."

"I will." Pat turned and started walking back to the hotel. I was a little envious in that moment that she lived the next town over and didn't have to make my fourteen-hour drive home. I sighed a little, knowing it would be some time before we saw each other again.

Turning my attention back to my departure, I clipped a fresh bucket of water to the side of each dog's crate, turned their fan on, and shut the door. I climbed into the driver's seat and looked through my audiobooks on a CD that I had rented from the library. I had already started *The Nightingale* by Kristin Hannah on my way there, so I popped it in and began where it left off. It was 9:00 a.m. Looking in my rearview mirror, I could see Manny sitting up in his crate.

"I'd lay down Manny. We've got a long day ahead of us." I put the truck in gear and started for home. "And away we go."

*1:00 p.m.*

I stopped and let the dogs stretch.

Used to these long-distance drives and always trying to eat as healthy as I could, I had packed some "road food"—apples, almonds, cheese, and crackers—to snack on. I would eat an actual meal when I got to the hotel. I grabbed an apple and took a bite, wiping the juice that slid out of the corner of my mouth with the back of my hand. I watched Manny and Tripp sniff through the grass.

Luckily, the rain had stopped a few hours ago, and we were making pretty good time. This would be the dogs' last out until we got to our hotel. We were on track to arrive before dark, barring no unforeseen circumstances.

*4:00 p.m.*

At 4:00 p.m., I heard the guitar strum of my phone's ringtone. I glanced at the display: "No caller ID."

*Why would anyone have that as a display*, I thought and didn't answer. A minute later it beeped alerting me that the "No caller ID" left a voicemail.

I pressed play as a man casually spoke. "Hi. My name is Deputy Brody. I'm calling from the Alameda County Sheriff's office in California. If you can please call me back." He left his number. "Thank you very much. Again, my name is Deputy Brody."

*Shit. I do not want to call this guy back.*

I knew it must have to do with Kevin since he was living in California, and I assumed he got arrested for something. Instead of calling Deputy Brody, I picked up the phone and called Tom.

"I think Kevin got arrested," I blurted out, completely aggravated when Tom picked up.

"What happened?" he asked.

"I got a message from the sheriff's office in California. The guy that left the message was a deputy. His voice sounded like it was no big deal but wanted me to call him back."

Tom never mentioned to me that day that he thought it was weird the police were calling the parents of someone who was twenty-five years old; he told me years later. I never made that connection.

"Ugh, I don't want to call," I said secretly hoping Tom would offer to call so I didn't have to deal with it.

"Just call the guy back. He probably got arrested." Tom was at his friend's house and didn't want to deal with the police.

"Okay. I just saw a sign for a New York state rest area. I'll pull over there."

"Okay. Call me back."

"'Kay. Bye." I hung up.

I hated that it was my turn to deal with Kevin being in trouble, but Tom was the one who handled putting up Kevin's bail money a few years prior when he was arrested for having marijuana; so technically, it was my turn.

Anytime Kevin got in trouble, I always started out being angry with him. Then, once I talked to him, I'd soften because he would always be so sorry, seeing how it affected Tom and me. I had a half dozen apology letters he had written us from his late teens and early twenties. It was like somehow, when he was in the middle of something, he couldn't see the consequence or potential danger coming. He had always been this way—that sweet childhood innocence had always been both a blessing and a curse. It was part of his charm, but as his mother, he was the one I worried about.

*I'm going to show him those apology letters when his kids are teenagers.*

As I pulled into the busy New York state rest area, a sickening dread had formed in my stomach.

*He just got a job working with autistic kids. How will this affect his job?*

I decided to park far from the brick building's entrance, having the sense I'd want privacy for this call. I pulled out my phone and re-listened to the voicemail.

It was 4:17 p.m.

*It's not even nighttime in California.*

I looked in the rearview mirror to see if the dogs were sitting up, but they weren't, indicating there wasn't any rush to let them out. And I wanted to get this phone call over with.

"I'll let you guys out in a few minutes," I told them, looking over my shoulder.

Both dogs were in their crates in the capped bed of my pickup truck with their fan on so they couldn't hear me.

My attention turned back to the phone call. I looked at the main screen on my phone, looking at the time again.

*This is an odd time to be arrested.*

I could feel my heart starting to pound and thought again back to that phone call from a few years ago. Kevin had been pulled over for driving with a headlight out. It was daytime then, too, and there was no need to have his lights on. When the police approached the car, they smelled the pot inside his car and searched it. He was subsequently arrested after the police found a bag of marijuana, which was not legal in New Hampshire at the time. Part of his court requirements were to attend a drug program and report to a probation officer.

*But if this is about marijuana, that doesn't make sense. Marijuana is legal in California, so why would he be in trouble even if he did have some pot on him? Plus, he doesn't have a car out there.*

I listened to the message again this time with a pen and paper, ready to take notes. Holding the phone, I took a few calming breaths and pressed into my dial pad the number the deputy left.

"Hello. You've reached the Alameda County Sheriff's Department. How can I help you?"

"Could I please speak to Deputy Brody?" I asked.

"May I ask who's calling?"

"Susan Lynch."

"Hold on, please."

There was a brief silence on the line, and I nervously doodled on the paper as I waited.

"Hello. This is Deputy Brody."

"Hi. This is Susan Lynch. You left me a message wanting me to call you back?"

"Oh, yes. Hi." He paused briefly before he asked, "Do you know a Kevin Lynch?"

"Yes," I said cautiously.

*"A" Kevin Lynch? Who says that?*

I instantly did not like this guy.

That mama bear defending her cub rose inside me.

Kevin was labeled early on in elementary school, not for having behavior problems, but for mostly being too social. He was well-liked by his peers, but several of his teachers felt they needed to keep him under their thumbs. I think the consensus was if they could keep him under wraps, the class would follow suit.

He was sometimes blamed for doing things he didn't do such as the time when the middle school principal called the house. She requested either Tom or me to come into the school to discuss an incident that happened on the school bus. Tom took that one and sat in the principal's office as she explained that Kevin drew a penis on the seat of the bus.

Tom listened very calmly as she proceeded to tell him that Kevin had used Whiteout for the drawing. Tom assured her Kevin wouldn't even know what Whiteout was, but she insisted a student saw Kevin do it. She said she considered the matter closed, but knowing the incident was out of character for Kevin, Tom asked her to call him if they found any new information. The principal did call Tom a week later to let him know they found out who had drawn on the seat and apologized. Tom told her she owed the apology to Kevin.

*What kind of question is "Do I know Kevin?" Of course, I know him. He told you I was his mother ... otherwise, how would you have gotten my phone number?*

"*How* do you know him?" was the question that snapped me out of my defensiveness and raised the hair on the back of my neck.

"I'm... his... mmmm-other," I stammered, "Why?" I said in barely a whisper.

*Please, please, please let him tell me Kevin was arrested. Or maybe he can tell me he was in a fender bender. Yes, a fender bender would be fine. He's still under our health insurance, so any stitches will be covered. Kevin should have his insurance card on him. Yes, he will have it. I always remind him to keep it in his wallet.*

"Kevin is dead," he said flatly.

The air was sucked out of my lungs, the car, the world, and I couldn't breathe. A trap door had just opened underneath me, and I was falling at lightning speed. Every muscle in my body was clenched tight trying to grab Kevin as if he was in front of me, but it was like trying to hold onto a cloud. I was gasping to catch my breath.

"Mrs. Lynch? Are you there?"

"What ...," I whispered.

I managed to get out the only thing I could think of: "... What do you mean?"

I knew the news was going to be bad, but I was a Universe away from ever thinking death.

"We don't know exactly what happened. He was at a friend's apartment; they had been partying and ..."

The details came in a series of bullets, and I could hardly hold onto the fractals of information that seemed to be speeding through the phone while everything else around me had come to a standstill.

At a friend's house.

Two kids with him.

Nothing suspicious was found.

They were drinking and smoking marijuana.

Empty Jameson bottle, a bong, and his backpack.

Friends found him at 8:00 a.m. on a futon.

They called 911 and attempted CPR.

Neither kid knows what happened.

The toxicology results will take four months.

"What do I do now?" I asked him. It was the only thing I thought to ask, and I don't even remember his answer.

All I knew was that I was afraid to hang up. He was my only connection who knew where Kevin was. I asked for his number again just to keep him on the phone a moment longer, then briefly explained I was on the road and had to call my husband and get home.

*I gotta call Tom. He always knows what to do in a crisis.*

Tom and I have been together since we were nineteen, and we have handled everything together since.

My hands shook as I hit favorites in my contacts. I pressed Tom's name right at the top. He picked up on the first ring.

"Tom, Tom," I croaked, barely containing the sob swelling in my throat. My hands were shaking so badly I almost dropped the phone, but I couldn't allow myself to fall apart. Not yet.

*I need to get home.*

"What happened?"

"Kevin is dead!" I blurted out, knowing there was no way to soften the blow.

"What!??"

I could hear the creaking of steps under his weight as he walked up a flight of stairs at his friend's house. I conveyed what few points the deputy had told me.

"Tell me again what is happening?" Tom asked in complete disbelief.

"Kevin is dead," I repeated, even though I couldn't understand it either.

In that moment, I did not have the luxury of coming undone—*I needed to get home ASAP.*

David Kessler, one of the world's foremost experts on grief and loss, talks about *touching the pain and taking a break* as a way to cope with the enormity of the loss. The idea is that we can't take in all of it at once—we acknowledge and feel it in small pieces and have to turn to something else. I would learn about this years later in a writing workshop on trauma and grief. At that moment, I couldn't do anything other than get home as quickly as possible to be with Tom.

We discussed me making the drive home by myself, and I assured him I could manage it. Seven hours was too long to wait for someone to come get me. My mind reverted to what I would normally do in a crisis: identify the immediate problem and figure out what I needed to do to solve it. The immediate problem was that I was seven hours away from home. I needed gas, to use the bathroom, and to potty the dogs.

I had parked next to the grassy area at the back of the parking lot, knowing somehow, I would need privacy for my phone call and thinking I would let the dogs have a romp. Opening the door to my truck, I realized how heavy my body had become. It was as if someone had slipped a lead blanket over my shoulders completely unnoticed while I was on the phone. I let the dogs out briefly to do their business and put them right back into the truck and fed them their dinner in their crates. They didn't make any fuss about the quick in and out, already sensing something was very wrong.

I lumbered to the brick A-frame building, glancing around to get a feel for where I was, and noticed a blue and white AMVETS Memorial Highway sign. For the rest of my life, that highway would be known to me as Death Road.

It was Saturday, and there was a steady stream of people funneling toward the entrance of the building. I stayed toward the outside of the crowd, but the entrance column was in my way and forced me to move closer to the group. I glanced up as I got to the door to see it was closing toward my face. The man who was just a few steps in front of me didn't hold the door.

Anger flickered in me.

*You have no idea what I just heard*, I thought sending the message telepathically to the back of his head and just as quickly let it go. All I had the bandwidth for was getting home. We walked as a group to the restrooms and divided at the "women" and "men" signs.

Everybody was too close to me. The entire building was set up where everyone was too close. Walking into the restroom, my senses were assaulted by the mingling smells of bleach, urine, and shit. A wave of nausea came over me as I walked past the yellow "slippery when wet" sign, watching my feet take small steps to get me to the toilet.

Leaving the stall, I took the same small, labored steps to the sinks to splash some cold water on my face. Between nausea and the wet floor, I was moving at a snail's pace when a woman, who was more confident of her ability to walk across the wet floor, brushed by my shoulder rushing past me. I was left feeling like she'd hit me with a hammer.

All my senses were heightened to levels I had never experienced before, and I couldn't leave the rest area fast enough. I walked as quickly as I could back out of the building and back to the cocoon that was my truck. I checked on Manny and Tripp to make sure they were still there. I was grateful they were looking like they were tired, which eased any guilt of not stopping for the night. We were going to push through the next seven hours to get home.

I left without getting gas as I wanted to put as much distance from that parking lot and me as possible. Getting behind the wheel of my truck, I knew I couldn't allow myself to think about Kevin or what had happened. I couldn't let any emotion in. Tom said he'd make the calls to his parents who lived close to us and to Matthew who was living in Montreal. I still had to call my parents, but first I needed to cancel my hotel.

*5:02 p.m.*

I had the number to the Red Roof Inn written down with the address in my notebook on the passenger seat. I dialed. An automated voice answered. "Thank you for calling Red Roof Inn in Syracuse. To speak to a hotel representative please dial zero or stay on the line." I pressed zero.

"Hello. It's a great day at the Red Roof Inn in Syracuse. My name is Derick. How can I help you?" he said, not at all convincing about it being a great day.

"I need to cancel a reservation."

"Okay. Your name and the arrival date?"

"Susan Lynch. I was supposed to arrive today."

"Oh. Okay."

He asked for a few details, which I provided.

"Okay. You're all set," he confirmed.

"Thank you. Bye." I hung up mentally checking off an item on the list and focusing on what was next.

*5:15 p.m.*

I found my mother's number in my contacts and pressed her name to call.

"Hi, Honey! Are you home from the National yet?" my mother asked, excited to hear the details.

I couldn't bear to hear the happiness in her voice.

"Are you sitting down?" I asked.

Hearing the tone of my voice, her own tone shifted. "Yes," she said with trepidation, "What's wrong?"

"Kevin is dead," I said, not recognizing the sound of my own voice at that moment.

"What? What?!"

I paused to give her a second to catch her breath.

"What did you say?!" she asked again.

I heard her repeating my words to my father, and I heard him in the background making a sound I've never heard before.

"Kevin is dead. I don't know many details. The kids don't know what happened. He went to bed drunk but otherwise fine. I don't know if it was his asthma. I'm driving home."

"Dad and I will come get you. Where are you?" she said, pleading with me to be off the road.

There was no way I was sitting idle and waiting for someone to come to get me. I knew how to drive. I just needed to keep my emotions at bay and out of all conversations so I could get home to Tom.

"Mom, I'm not waiting for someone to get me. I can do it. Tom's calling Matthew and his parents. I gotta call Milly and Stew. I'll call you in a little bit."

"Don't call me. Concentrate on driving. Are you sure we can't come and get you?"

"No, I'm not waiting."

There was nothing left to say, and she didn't want me distracted on the phone.

"I love you. Be careful," she added as if trying to cast some sort of invisible safety net over me, but those words skipped in my chest as I remembered they were the same words I said to Kevin just days before; and they didn't work.

"I love you, too, Mom."

*5:40 p.m.*

I pulled off the highway to get gas.

Manny was entered in an upcoming American Kennel Club tracking test, and the test secretary had emailed me the day before confirming we got into the test. I pulled up the email on my phone, hit reply, and wrote:

*I need to scratch from the TD test. Thank you,*
*Susan Lynch*

I hit "send," opened the door, and moved my leaden body out of the truck. I put my credit card in and lifted the pump handle with my head down, not wanting to make any eye contact with anyone. On the opposite side of the gas pump, I saw someone else's shoes pointing slightly inward as they stood waiting for their tank to fill.

*You have no idea what I just heard.*

*6:00 p.m.*

Milly and Stew were good friends who happened to live two streets away. Milly and I met in 2007 at a hunt test and had been training partners ever since, spending five days a week together, then sharing dinners with our husbands on the weekends. The four of us were tight, and I needed to call them and let them know before they heard it somewhere else. Like any small town, news spreads fast.

I took a deep breath and called Milly.

"Hey," she said, cheerfully, also eager to know about my results.

"Are you sitting down?" I asked.

"Yes, we're driving. We just picked up a new sofa."

"Are *you* driving?"

"No, Stew is. What's up?"

"I just got the news that Kevin is dead."

"What?!"

She would later tell me she motioned for Stew to pull over so she could vomit on the side of the road.

"A deputy called me from California and said Kevin was dead, but they don't know any details as to how it happened."

43

"Where are you?"

"In New York, on Route 90."

"We'll come get you."

"No, I can't wait, I just need to get home."

She hung up and they headed to my house to be with Tom.

*6:30 p.m.*

Tom called to check in.

"I'm okay. I just got gas."

"My brothers and parents are here. I just called my brother, Michael, who was on his way, but I called him and told him not to come. There's nothing anyone can do."

"I keep looking in my rearview mirror, but I haven't seen the dogs sit up once," I told him.

"Good. Did you feed them yet?"

"Yes."

"Okay. Someone just came in. I'll call you in a little while."

"Okay. Bye."

"Bye."

*7:00 p.m.*

I looked down when I heard my phone ring and saw that it was my friend, Alison. Alison was an active member of Yankee Golden Retriever Club and had been helping me for the past several months train Manny for a tracking test. We had been emailing back and forth for the past week, trying to nail down a day to go out the following week to train since the test was only two weeks away.

I answered the phone "Hi, Alison."

"Hi! I just wanted to check in to see what you were thinking for next week?"

"Alison, Kevin died this morning."

"What?? What happened?"

"We don't know. He had asthma, but he was drinking, too. They don't know."

"Oh my God. What can I do?"

"Can you please email Yankee's Board of Directors to let them know that I won't be at the meeting on Tuesday night? I'm also chairing the judge's clinic at the end of the month. Mostly everything is all set for that, but I'm just making them aware."

"Of course. Oh my God. I am so sorry."

*7:30 p.m.*

Tom called for another check-in. "Hi."

"Hi."

"You doing okay?" he asked.

"Yeah."

"I convinced everyone to leave. It's hard with everyone here standing around. There's nothing to say," he said.

"I know."

"Are you still listening to your book?" he asked.

"Yeah, in between calls. It's something to focus on, and it's dark. It's about the holocaust."

"What's the name of it?"

"*The Nightingale*," I said flatly.

"Oh ... I think I'll watch some TV."

There was a moment of silence.

"What time is the GPS saying for arrival home?" he wanted to know.

I glanced at the GPS. "11:33 p.m."

"Okay, I'll call you in a while."

*8:15 p.m.*

Tom rang me again.

"Hi. The organ donor people called. They said Kevin had checked off as a donor on his license. They want to know if we are okay with it," he said.

"If he had it on there, I think we have to honor his wishes." I replied, completely baffled we were even having this conversation.

"Me, too," said Tom. "Okay. Let me call them back. You okay?"

"Yea. He'd be glad we said 'yes.'" I said thinking out loud.

I had only known for four hours that my baby boy was no longer alive. I hadn't arrived home yet. *IT* hadn't become real yet. And yet we were already having to make decisions about his body.

"Yeah, but I'm not sure why they are asking us since it's on his license. I'll call you in a bit," he said.

"Okay. Lemme know what they say."

We hung up.

I just needed to get home.

*8:20 p.m.*

Welcome to Massachusetts

*9:10 p.m.*

Tom called once more to update me.

"Hi. I left a message, but they haven't called me back yet. There are a bunch of questions they have to ask," he sighed.

"Oh. Weird that they are open. Although I guess they need to get them as it happens."

"Yup."

"What are you doing?" I asked.

"Watching *The Hunt for Red October* for the second time. This time without the sound."

"Huh?"

"Yeah, the sound was annoying me."

*10:15 p.m.*

I happened to glance down, the light on my phone casting a small glow across Tom's photo before it started to ring.

"Hi," I answered.

"They still haven't called me back," he said. "Maybe it will be tomorrow."

*11:40 p.m.*

Welcome to New Hampshire

*11:42 p.m.*

I turned onto my street, feeling like I had been gone a year. This was home, yet nothing was the same. It was dark out, but at that moment, it would have been okay if the sun never rose again. I couldn't imagine a new day with the sun shining and no Kevin. It would be the greatest offense.

I let the dogs out to do their business, and we walked into the house. It was almost midnight, and I was grateful they were calm. Tom walked into the kitchen with his phone to his ear and held up a finger indicating "one minute." The one finger raised in the air has always stuck with me. I had just driven fourteen hours, seven of them after hearing the worst news of my life, and when I got home, I couldn't just go to my husband. The business side of death couldn't, didn't, wouldn't wait.

Tom wrote on a Post-it he had been on the phone for the past forty-five minutes with the organ donor people and didn't want to repeat the whole process. They were asking questions only Kevin could answer—things like whether he had had sex within the last two weeks with someone from out of the country.

I heard Tom say "I don't know" for the next twenty minutes as I moved between inside and outside, taking bags and equipment from the truck and leaving everything in a heap on the kitchen floor.

Because he was found dead, he was not able to donate his organs. They were, however, able to use his corneas, heart valves, skin, and long bones from his legs. The very last question they asked was if we wanted to be contacted by the donor recipients. I didn't know what to say when Tom covered the mouthpiece of the phone to ask my opinion.

"I don't know. That is a big decision," I said.

"Anonymous," Tom said into the phone.

A few moments later and several more questions, Tom hung up.

We were now just the two of us, holding this weight we had been handed.

Up until then, I hadn't had the luxury of falling apart. I had only allowed myself to give attention to the *to-do list* and get myself safely home. Now, there I was, in my living room, and the enormity of what just happened hit me, making my legs buckle. Tom and I clung to each other and sobbed.

*What do I do now?*

That single question echoed what I had asked Deputy Brody, but this time I was asking the Universe. "What do I do now?" was the million-dollar question I would spend the next five years trying to answer.

# Chapter 4

# The Final Tour

*October 4–10, 2015*

I don't remember what happened between falling apart in Tom's arms and going to bed that night. I just knew Matthew was on a Greyhound bus home from Montreal as I slept, set to arrive early the next morning.

When I opened my eyes the following day, Tom had already left to pick him up from the bus station thirty minutes away. For one brief moment, in that blink between sleeping and waking, everything was fine. But then I remembered. This forgetting and remembering would happen each morning for months.

Manny and Tripp came over to me and sat alongside the bed. Manny rested his chin inches from my face, getting a good look at me.

"Hi, Manny." I touched the soft fur on his ear, then slid my fingertips to stroke the side of his face as he looked at me intently. I reached for the box of tissues, and he laid down next to my bed as if he could now relax, having discovered I had made it through the night.

I blew my nose and dragged myself out of bed, heading for the kitchen to make a pot of coffee. I was on autopilot, going through the morning routine with the dogs in tow. Both trotted past me when I opened the door to let them out, and I watched them in a daze as both heads went down to the grass to sniff out what new smells from nighttime critters had crossed through their yard overnight.

My thoughts had been a continuous reel revolving around the news, now only fifteen hours old. Seeing Tom's car pull up the driveway, returning from the bus station, brought me to the edge of a new horror. Until that moment, I hadn't given Matthew's loss my attention. Tom and I had been adrift in this new sea of grief, and now I was watching Matthew step out of the car to his new world as an only child. He looked as if he had aged ten years in just one day. I walked out the door and toward him with my arms wide, and he walked into them. We stood quietly for a moment in our embrace until he pulled away.

"I made a pot of coffee."

The three of us walked into the house and straight to the kitchen.

Tom poured himself a cup of coffee and sat at the kitchen table with his laptop to start looking for a funeral home. He tapped something into the search bar, then leaned back in his chair as he began to scan results.

I linked my hands around my mug. "What do you even look for?" I asked. I couldn't believe we were sitting around the family dinner table, picking out a funeral home.

"Online reviews," he said and kept typing, scrolling, and clicking, moving between websites.

While he scrolled and clicked and Matthew lost himself inside his own laptop screen, I kept looking from one of them to the other like I may never see them again. I couldn't bring myself to do anything other than just sit there and stare at them.

Moments later, Tom's mouse stopped moving, and I watched his eyes scanning the screen.

"I found one. Davis is the name. People seem to like them," Tom said, pointing at the laptop where I assumed people had left comments about their experiences. The name sounded familiar.

"I think that's the one Pat used when her father died. I'm pretty sure they were happy with them," I said.

Tom disappeared briefly to call them and returned moments later. "I left a voicemail."

Ten minutes passed, and Tom's phone was ringing.

Tom answered. "Hello? Hi, Andy. Thank you for calling me back so quickly ... Yes, my son's name is Kevin Lynch ... He died yesterday ... He's at the Alameda coroner's office in Oakland, California ... Yes, they are doing an autopsy ... Okay. Tomorrow at 11:00 a.m. ... Thank you. Bye."

Matthew lifted his head up from his laptop, "Kevin's Facebook page is blowing up."

Tom and I crowded around Matthew's screen to read the posts.

One after another we scrolled through pictures and stories posted by his friends, expressing what Kevin meant to them. They seemed to go on for pages and pages, and they were the only things that brought us any comfort.

In one picture, Kevin and two of his friends had walked up to the famous home of the Grateful Dead at 710 Ashbury Street in San Francisco. The gate happened to be unlocked and they took it upon themselves to sit on the steps and have someone take their picture. Kevin was beaming in the photo. His hair was long but tied back, and he was wearing gray and brown corduroy shorts and strapped sandals. Except for his white Ninja Turtles t-shirt, he looked very much like he belonged at this famous home from the 1960s. When I saw the photo date, I realized it was taken the very same day Kevin and I shared our last phone call.

The next morning, we made the short seven-mile drive from our house to the city of Nashua. The sun was shining so brightly it felt offensive. We drove along familiar roads— familiar roads that only drudged up memory after memory of Kevin.

On any normal day, I would drive on these roads to get local produce at Lull Farm where Kevin worked. On a normal day, these roads would take me past the Catholic church that Kevin was confirmed in. On a normal day, these roads would get me to the grocery store where Kevin would toss his favorite snacks in the carriage over the years.

Today was not a normal day.

We wouldn't go to any of those places. We would continue driving past Lull Farm, past the church, and past the grocery store. We would continue until we reached a white antique house with green shutters and a small sign on the front lawn that read "Davis Funeral Home est.1842."

The funeral home was a landmark perched at the point of a fork in the road like it didn't want you to miss it, yet we had to drive another one-hundred yards to find the parking lot. It's the second oldest funeral home in New Hampshire, which could explain why the parking lot seemed like an afterthought.

I began to wonder if Davis was a good choice.

*Maybe people won't know where to park? Maybe when they can't find the parking lot, they will just turn around and go home? Maybe nobody will come.*

There was a feeling of reverence walking across the threshold. How many parents had been here before us? We were the only two standing in the foyer, yet the low ceiling gave the space a crowded feel. I could see the chairs lined on every wall of the next room.

*That must be where everyone gathers.*

Formal pictures of men in dark suits in elaborate gold frames lined the walls of the staircase. The funeral home was more than 170 years old, and I would have thought it looked more like a New England inn if it wasn't for a few odd details. The pew in the back of the room was set under an archway with two tall lamps and long drapes. Andy, the funeral director, snapped me out of my assessment with his hand extended for me to shake.

*When did he walk in?*

We all shook hands and made our introductions.

Andy had already assured us he was working with the funeral home in California, and Kevin's body would be arriving on Wednesday. We followed him up the stairs that creaked in protest under our weight. Andy guided us into a room I could only assume was the standard place to first converse with the family of the deceased.

The three of us sat at a large boardroom-type table while Andy guided us through the business side of death: wake and funeral arrangements; preparation and filing notices; authorizations; consents; and transportation of the body from the airport, to and from the church for the services, then to the cremation facility. We were told it was important to get multiple copies of the death certificate. Then came the cost discussion. There were additional fees for the medical examiner, funeral home in California, and his flight back to New Hampshire.

Andy then asked us whether we wanted him cremated before or after the church service.

"What difference does it make?" I asked.

"Traditionally the Catholic church wants the body intact when it is in the church. If you choose to do that, Kevin's body will return here until Monday when we will take him to the crematorium," Andy said.

"Oh," I said, and Tom nodded. There were so many things to know that I didn't want to. So many decisions to make that I didn't want to make.

I was raised Catholic, so we agreed to have the casket come into the church before cremation.

Andy was trying to be as delicate as possible. "You will need to bring me clothes to dress him in."

"He doesn't have a suit," I said. Up until then, I had only ever seen men in suits in a coffin. Kevin owned about thirty tie-dye t-shirts, cargo shorts, and hoodie sweatshirts with Phish patches. These were not clothes you would wear to church.

"He can be in whatever clothes you would like. It doesn't have to be a suit," Andy reassured me.

"Really?" I asked, relieved.

"Yes, I've had families bring me their loved one's favorite fishing shirt and flies pinned to their favorite hat. I encourage people to personalize their loved one's clothing." This put me at ease. I couldn't imagine seeing Kevin in anything other than his colorful tie dyes and flip flops. He wasn't one to conform in this life, and I didn't want to send him off to the next looking as if he did.

The final detail was to choose a coffin. We all got up from the table and followed Andy into the adjacent room where the busts of coffins were on display. Each had a side card with the prices and the features. He gave us a few moments to discuss which we'd like. The final question was if we wanted to rent a nicer coffin, then put him in a "greener" one to be cremated in.

"No, I don't want him to move twice." *He's been through enough.*

"Okay. I'll let you walk around and talk about it. When you're done, come to my office downstairs, and let me know what you've decided on." He turned and left us alone.

The most important thing for me was that he was resting comfortably when I saw him for the last time. At every wake I'd ever been to, I saw the head on a pillow with cushioning around the body. That's how I wanted to send Kevin off as he embarked on the next phase of his journey.

The drive home from the funeral home was filled with thoughts on what I was going to choose for him to wear. Andy had given me permission to personalize his clothes. I didn't want to be disrespectful, but at the same time, I wanted him to look like him.

Back at home, I headed straight for Kevin's bedroom to wade through his closet and start rummaging through his clothes. By Tuesday afternoon, after much deliberation, I had an outfit picked out for him. Kevin was thrifty with his money and would often go to second-hand stores when shopping for clothes. The last Christmas he was home, he had bought a brown vest with large, wool patches on the front. I had hidden my oh-my-God face and just smiled when he walked into the kitchen. He looked proud as punch as the palms of his hands smoothed down the front of his vest.

"Do you like my new vest?" he asked with a smile so big it said *You know you do.*

"Wow, Kev, sharpie guy," I said, winking at him. "Sharpie guy" was a term the kids used when they were little to describe when they were in dress clothes during holidays or family weddings.

"You look great."

"What?" he said. Kevin almost always said "what" when he was given compliments. It was like he wanted to hear them twice.

"You look great," I repeated. I smiled, knowing his vest would get him a few more "sharpie guy" comments from his grandparents. Later that evening, at my in-laws for Christmas Eve, we had our last Christmas picture taken together with him in the brown vest, sitting on the couch with our arms linked. I wanted to keep the vest since it held memories of our last Christmas together, so I opted not to use it.

There were only three button-down shirts in his closet. One was plain light blue, the one he wore for his court date after his arrest for marijuana possession. That one was a hard "no." The two others were multi-colored stripes he had bought at Savers, the local thrift store. I picked the maroon, blue, and yellow striped one. The pants were gray, wide-wale corduroys. I also picked two different socks—one black and one white—in honor of his signature style. He hated wearing shoes, so I chose not to include any.

* * *

On Wednesday, Tom took the clothes to the funeral home. Andy came out of his office to tell Tom that Kevin's body had still not been delivered from San Francisco. He was to be embalmed out there before he was flown to New Hampshire, but there was some snafu about needing a signature for the body to be released from the coroner's office.

When Tom arrived back home, I looked at him expectantly. After twenty-seven years of marriage, I knew the look on his face when he had unpleasant news. Normally, when he was in a "get things done" mode, his gray blue eyes would meet mine directly to address what we needed to tackle next, but he just stood there, pensively rubbing his goatee.

"What's the matter?" I asked.

"Kevin hasn't arrived yet," he mumbled.

My eyes went wide with disbelief. "Are you fucking kidding me?! What do you mean? I am going to call the coroner's office."

He snapped back into his "get things done" mode. "No, don't. Let me do it," he said, trying to calm me down.

"Tom, the wake is already announced. It's happening in two days, and he's not even here." I was panicking for the services but also for fear they wouldn't give him back to me.

"I know. I'll handle it," Tom said.

To his credit, he calmly but firmly told the person at the coroner's office they needed to sign today so we could hold the services. The office assured him they would get the signature by the end of the day.

On Thursday, Kevin's girlfriend, Kacey, flew in from California. He had been living with her for a few months, but we hadn't had the chance to meet her yet. When she arrived at our home, it was like seeing a beloved family member for the first time in a long while. Right away, I could sense the kindness that Kevin mentioned when he spoke of her. Her slim frame was wrapped in shades of brown and green with silver artisan earrings dangling from her ears. She radiated an earthy calm. Her demeanor drew me in, and her stories of Kevin held me captivated as she spoke of their day-to-day life together. She gave a sad smile as she reminisced about the rainbow they saw on their way to pick up a pizza the night before he died but then gave a small chuckle when she got to the part where Kevin had slowed the car down and was looking out the window saying, "Oh my gosh. It's just so bright and distracting!" We had all agreed it was so typical of Kevin to savor the fleeting moment of a rainbow.

By the time Kacey made it to our house, Tom had already been working on the photo boards. Boxes of photos and posters covered the kitchen table. She joined him and started asking questions and pointing at specific pictures from when he was little. When there was a break in their conversation, Tom explained his method for grouping the photos for the boards and she offered to help. Working side by side, they bonded over shared stories about Kevin as they arranged the pictures. It was a near perfect moment except for the fact that Kevin wasn't with us.

Tom printed out some of the pictures his friends had posted on his Facebook wall along with some of our favorites of their comments like "A person who shines so bright you only need to meet him once to know how incredible we have the potential to be." There were dozens of comments all attesting to the love and kindness that Kevin had shown them and a dozen more hilarious stories and photos of Kevin just being Kevin.

One of the photos Tom selected showed a printed picture of Kevin attached to a stick. This was from the summer of 2015. Kevin's favorite music festival was an annual event in Vermont called Frendly Gathering where they misspell "friend" to emphasize there's no "i" in "frend." Kevin was living in California and wasn't able to attend that year. When his friend, Keith, found out he wouldn't be there, he had a photo of Kevin made into a life-sized cardboard image and attached it to a wooden stick. Kevin's friends carried stick-Kevin around with them all weekend, even propping it up on stage when Twiddle, one of his favorite bands, played their set. I imagined briefly that the band might pull stick-Kevin out for their next show in his honor. I'd never know, of course, as my only connection to them was Kevin, and now he was gone.

That afternoon, Tom got a call from Andy saying Kevin's body would be arriving at Logan Airport in the morning. They would have enough time to do what they needed to do to get him ready for the wake Friday afternoon.

"Don't you think it's funny that Kevin arrives at his own wake just in the nick of time?" I said not at all laughing. "This is 100% a Kevin thing to do even though he's not actually responsible for being late."

"I was just thinking the same thing," Tom said.

The dogs were used to lots of physical activity and, at the very least, needed me to keep up with their daily hikes in the woods. Walking with them those few days was a way to briefly escape all the *doing*. I also felt the dogs might need a break from being so vigilant with all the extra attention they were giving me, but I would soon learn they wouldn't relent.

I loaded the dogs up into the truck and headed to a local trail a couple miles away. I always walked them off leash, and they always stayed slightly ahead of me. Today was no exception other than they now were stopping to look back, making sure I was there more often than normal.

When I came home, I was grateful to see Milly had delivered our laundry all washed and had made the dinner that was on the counter. I walked past it to check out Tom and Kacey's progress on the photo boards. Upon seeing me,

Kacey walked over to her bag, pulled out a gray t-shirt, and carefully handed it to Tom.

I thought it was one of Kevin's until she said, "Kevin bought this for you."

Tom held the shirt gently in his hands for a moment savoring the gift he was just given from beyond the grave. He then spread it across the kitchen table to read the words "DAD, perfect to a tee" in navy blue embroidery. Next to the words was a single golf ball perched on a tee.

"We were thrift shopping, and when Kevin found this shirt, he laughed and said, 'I have to get this for my dad. He loves golf.'"

Tom had played many rounds of golf with Kevin when he was growing up but hardly ever played golf without Kevin. Part of what was so moving was that Kevin had made the assumption about Tom's love of the sport merely based on their time spent playing together.

"Kevin had put it up to the front of his chest and asked if I thought it would fit his Dad. He had clearly forgotten I'd never met Tom before," Kacey said with a faint smile of recollection.

I glanced up from the shirt to see Tom's shoulders shaking up and down. Before this week, it would have been strange to see Tom sob.

● ● ●

The next day was Friday, the day of the wake. I took Andy's suggestion of customizing the services and asked Kacey if she would select some of Kevin's favorite music from his iPod to be played softly during the wake. My friend, Donna, had compiled photos of Kevin and had a hardcover photo guestbook that was displayed at the entrance. Tom, Matthew, and I arrived at the funeral home a little early so we could see Kevin's body before people started to arrive.

It had started raining, and we assumed people would be on-time to avoid waiting in line in the rain. When we walked into the funeral home, Andy was there to greet us and take our jackets. After hanging up our coats he stood at the curtained double doors that were the entrance to the receiving room. He extended his arm into the room and gave a thin smile and a nod of his head. Matthew chose to hang back and let Tom and me go in first.

It was the first time we had seen Kevin since we got on separate planes at the airport in Costa Rica seven months ago. He was slightly propped up in the casket with a slight smile on his face. He was in that colorful striped button-down shirt with his hair pulled back. The bottom half of the casket was closed so you couldn't see his gray corduroys or his mismatched socks, but we knew they were there. Resting atop the bottom half of the casket was his favorite Nantucket red baseball cap signed by all four Twiddle band members and the framed bulletin board my friend, Milly, used to display his festival tickets and cloth wristbands. She couldn't fit all that he had saved, but among some of his favorite shows were the two tickets for the Grateful Dead's Fare Thee Well tour displayed right in the center.

I was relieved that he looked comfortable. I'd seen him lying down with his eyes closed a thousand times.

*Yes, he's just sleeping.* This was my strategy for getting through the next four hours.

I felt satisfied that Kevin would have approved of the details marking his final tour in this world. He would be happy with me—with what he was wearing, the music coming from his iPod playing, and photos of some of his great memories with family and friends. He would be happy that all the parts of his twenty-five years and two months were represented in the photo boards and would be loving what people had written about him. I'm sure he'd already read them at least twice.

Tom and I stood and turned to see Matthew—his eyes fixated on the coffin as he walked past us. It was his turn to say goodbye. Matthew had spent most of the week in his room, writing the eulogy, and when he did come out, he had made it clear he didn't want to talk about Kevin. He also did not want to stand with Tom and me while people gave their condolences. "No" was his swift and direct reply when we asked, leaving no room for discussion, so we dropped it. He spent the entire evening in a chair, off to the side of the room, looking as if he wanted to be alone.

There were dozens of flower arrangements, but one, a large bouquet of yellow roses, stood out because of the color. When I looked to see who had sent it, the card simply read "Love, The Minions." Kevin had affectionately called his young cousins from the Costa Rica trip his little Minions from the animated movie of the same name.

Tom and I stood side by side next to the coffin, receiving condolences from a few hundred people for the next four hours. It was raining outside; the line was out the door the entire evening. I needn't have worried; people didn't let the parking or the weather deter them.

Family and friends were sharing stories, and those were the moments I wanted to bask in. A familiar-looking woman came through the line and gently put her hands over mine. I knew I should probably know her name, but I couldn't come up with it.

"Thank you for coming," I said.

She smiled at me and asked, "Do you know who I am?"

When I didn't answer her right away, she said, "I'm Sam Linden's mother."

Sam Linden had died tragically ten years ago in a car accident when he was sixteen years old. He was a year older than Kevin, so they knew each other but didn't hang around together.

Upon hearing his name, I was thrust back in time, standing in line at Sam's wake. I remember vividly looking at the photo boards they had made of him. They had a lake house, and I remembered looking at Sam in each of the pictures, jumping off the dock, riding a jet ski, waterskiing, and fishing. I remember the moment I realized *I have all the same photos of my own kids.*

Ten years later, she was in front of me at my son's wake.

She gave me a knowing hug and told me to reach out to her anytime. "It's a hard road," she said.

I wiped my eyes and nodded.

People continued to approach us in line, and at one point, I had heard Matthew laugh. I knew it was his voice but couldn't see him through the crowd. It would be years before I knew the details of that moment.

He had been sitting alone, and my sister had gone over to sit with him.

It was a gutsy move to ask someone so deep in grief, but she went for it. "Wanna hear something funny?" she asked.

He turned to look at her. "Um, yes?" he said, not at all sure she would have anything funny to say given the circumstances.

"So, I was poking around Kevin's Facebook page and was looking at people he follows and general information. I saw the 'About Kevin' section and clicked on it."

Matthew was now looking at the floor waiting for the punchline.

Lynne had started to giggle "You know what it said?" not waiting for his answer she replied, "I'm kind of a big deal."

That was the point when I heard him laugh and rightfully assumed someone had told him a funny story about Kevin that allowed him a moment of levity.

Lynne was happy he took it the way she had intended. "That is such a Kevin thing to say, right?!" Lynne said, smiling.

She said he was smiling and nodding, wiping his eyes.

* * *

The funeral was the next morning on Saturday. I had managed to pick out something appropriate for Kevin to wear, and now it was my turn. When Kevin was little, I was a substitute teacher in the elementary school. He had made a point to tell me he didn't want me to wear black when I was teaching. He said, "It makes the teacher look mean."

I was at the very beginning of trusting what I felt was right for me. I was glad I had the courage to have Kevin in his colorful shirt and decided I would also buck tradition and not wear black. I pushed past the hangers of black garments and stopped at a bright green blazer. Tom liked my choice of green, and that was good enough for me.

Before the funeral mass, Tom, Matthew, my parents, in-laws, and I went to the funeral home for what they call the final viewing. I knew I wanted to be the last to view his body and told everyone to start, to go ahead of me. When I had gone through his drawers earlier that week, I found letters I had sent him over the years. I found the one I sent him before he left for college and the one I gave him on his eighteenth birthday. I was so touched to learn he had saved them. After everyone had said their final goodbye, it was my turn. I could feel my hands shaking, holding one last letter to give him. I knelt before the casket.

Just peeking out the top of his chest pocket shirt was a little green cartoon character that was the mascot of the band Twiddle. Kevin's friend, Ryan, had slipped it in there, wanting to send him off with a little piece of the music that they loved so much.

"I love you sooooo much, Kev. Please give me a sign to let me know you are okay. I *need* to know you are okay."

I took in my final look at his beautiful face and kissed his forehead "Doooood night," I said softly and tucked the letter I wrote to him in beside him. I watched my tears fall into the coffin, remembering how he used to say goodnight as a three-year-old.

When he was little, I'd get him to go to bed by racing him up the stairs to his room. When he beat me to his bed, he'd hug me and say, "Doooood night, Mommy" because he couldn't make the hard "g" sound yet. We both continued to say it that way as a joke when he was growing up, even occasionally in his teen years.

My eyes filled with tears as they lingered on the Grateful Dead's Fare Thee Well tickets displayed front and center.

*Fare Thee Well, my love.*

I turned around and quickly headed for the exit.

Tom, Matthew, and I arrived at the church before the hearse. My parents and in-laws were walking into the church, and Matthew got out of the car to join them. Tom and I stayed sitting in the car, attempting to brace ourselves for the next step, which was the funeral mass. The hearse pulled up to the doors of the church, but I couldn't move. I didn't know what exactly I would experience, but I knew it was going to be excruciating. My body was defending my mind by not moving toward it.

"We gotta go in," Tom said quietly.

"I don't want to," I said with tears springing to my eyes once again.

*If I don't go in, it can't actually happen.*

"I don't either, but we have to."

Tom and I walked across the parking lot and greeted six of Kevin's friends who were waiting outside the entrance of the church. They, along with Matthew, were to be the pallbearers. Several of them had opted to wear the Grateful Dead tie-dye t-shirts versus a button-down under their suit jacket. We watched the casket be put onto a rolling rack of sorts, and when it was set, the boys took their places alongside the coffin.

The priest led the way down the center aisle with the pallbearers behind, guiding the casket to the front of the church. Tom and I, with our families behind us, followed them toward the altar and to the front pews.

Tom, Matthew, and I sat in the very front row of the church, something I'd never done in all the years I attended mass. I'd been raised Catholic and went to church throughout my childhood and into my late teens, but when I got married, I became lax about going. My mother, who was sitting in the pew behind us, passed me a box of tissues. I half-listened to the priest, hoping I would find his words comforting, but they fell short. After preparing the Eucharist, the priest was joined by two other members of the church to offer communion. They each took their places at the altar. I heard the first notes of "Here I Am, Lord" on the organ.

I watched family and friends walk up to the altar, receive communion, turn around, and walk by the coffin, gliding their fingers down the length of it. After everyone was seated, the priest, put the chalices away. Then he leaned toward the microphone. "Kevin's brother, Matthew, would like to say a few words."

With that announcement, Matthew stood and walked to the lectern. He cleared his throat and began to speak as if he were talking only to Kevin, leaving us all feeling as if we were listening in on a private conversation. Until now, he had not shared his feelings with anyone. And he never did again.

"Brother, I was listening to the Grateful Dead today. Remember this one?"

Matthew began to *sing* lines from the song "The Music Never Stopped" ...

"Brother! Remember that last day of surfing in Costa Rica? Remember the big, full, red sun that was setting on the ocean? Remember how it was behind a thin cloud so you could look right at it and how it lit up the sky with reds and yellows over the palm trees? There were barely any waves left, so I wasn't sure what our purpose was out there; but I was happy to be floating around with you. And you loved it; you packed surfing into every free minute that you had that week. Even when the water was flat, you bobbed around on your board, happy to chat with me or to scope out and talk to those pretty girls, so few of whom actually spoke any English. And they all loved you, of course, because you could express with your eyes and body language those good vibrations that words could only wish to communicate. And when the waves came, you paddled with rhythm, popping up, crouching, and turning with a style that you had already made your own.

By sunset on the seventh day, you were catching even the smallest waves and surfing with a proficiency and uniqueness that others would take weeks or months to acquire. Some others would never even get in the water, perfectly content to watch people like you from the beach. Which is fine, of course, but it's the soul of the surfers that my favorite books are written about. These are the characters whose lives are works of art, the ones that show us how life can be exquisitely beautiful and inspire us to demand more out of our own lives.

You inspire me, Kevin, with your free, sincere, empathetic soul—the soul that propelled you to drive across the country in sixty hours, to go off the grid, to work with special needs kids, to virtually go without sleep during so many multi-day music festivals with names like the Gathering of the Vibes or the Frendly Gathering.

You inspire me, Kevin, with your absolute confusion when instead of a seventh hour of swimming, I wanted to take a nap, with your flight home to surprise Mom for her birthday, with your flips off O'Toole's, with your donations of time and money to your network of homeless friends throughout Canada and the United States, with your complete disregard of the status quo and your bravery to do so. You inspire me, Kevin, with your soul of a romantic dog with the best kind of temperament....

And in that last conversation, you mentioned that your phone was running low on batteries and that the call would cut out eventually. I told you that I liked it better like that, and you agreed. You always had a tremendous capacity to embrace the unknown, the unexpected, and the absurd. Always going with the flow, always talking on a phone with a low battery. Why stretch out a conversation into three hours when you can burn bright in a conversation of thirty-seven minutes and thirty-four seconds? ...

Your ripple has been set into motion and will forever positively affect the Universe … Brother! May your perception always be positive, and may you find in the stars a paradise at least as good as the one that you perceived on this earth. I love you, Kevin, and I could not be prouder or more grateful to have you as my brother."

The only other sounds were sniffing and an occasional nose being blown as Matthew walked back to his seat. The priest stood up, wiped away his tears, and returned to the lectern.

"There will be a luncheon served at Alpine Grove immediately following the mass. The burial will be private and at a later time," the priest said.

The organ started up again, playing "Amazing Grace," as the pallbearers got up and wheeled the coffin back down the aisle.

I stood in the pew and turned to face an entire crowd of tear-stained faces and saw my grief reflected in them. We followed the coffin down the aisle and out of the church. Friends and family filtered out of the church behind us, tissues in hand. The mid-day sun was shining down on us, and people were hiding their swollen eyes behind sunglasses. Everyone was talking about how moving Matthew's eulogy was.

I overheard someone saying "I never had the pleasure of meeting Kevin, but I feel like I know him after hearing Matthew's eulogy."

The church bell started to gong, declaring it noon but had an ominous feel as the men from the funeral home loaded the casket back into the hearse. They placed a cloth over the casket, but it sloped at an angle, unstraight, untidy.

I took it upon myself to straighten and smooth it out before they closed the doors.

As the hearse drove away, I broke away from the crowd and walked alone down the sidewalk to get closer to the street. That long black car with curtains over the windows held my baby in it, and I'll never lose sight of it in my mind. I watched the hearse until it went out of sight, and when I couldn't see it anymore, I collapsed on the stone bench and wailed by myself.

Tom walked down the sidewalk, knowing I needed encouragement to come back up and say goodbye to people who wouldn't be going to the luncheon. We solemnly walked back up to the people who were waiting to say goodbye.

When we were done there, Tom, Matthew, and I walked across the parking lot to our car where I had left my cell phone. I saw I had missed a call from Graeme, my friend and the professional handler who showed Manny in conformation. Unbeknownst to me, he had driven seven hours that morning from Canada just to be at the funeral, to give me a hug of support. He was hoping to see me after the service but knew it wasn't the right time when the hearse had left. He hadn't planned on attending the luncheon as he needed to get back on the road to make the trip back home. I was overwhelmed at the outpouring of love and support.

On the way to the banquet hall, I had called my friend who offered to let my dogs out and check on them.

"They're doing fine," she said. "They've pottied, and I'm just now throwing a ball for them."

I thanked her and hung up as we arrived.

We walked into the facility with my parents and in-laws. Some people were standing, watching a projector displaying photos of Kevin on a screen.

*How can I be surrounded by people yet feel so utterly alone?*

Everyone wanted to know what they could do for me to soften my pain. Other than wanting Kevin back, all I wanted was to hear more stories of how much he meant to people. I needed to know they loved him deeply.

But living in the space between those moments of story sharing and the outpouring of love and support was the ever-present elephant in the room of how did he die? Some people asked, and some didn't. "What happened?" and "I don't know" were phrases that went together. We wouldn't know officially until the toxicology report came back.

I had forgotten about my green jacket until someone asked me about it at the reception. "What's with the color?" she said.

"Kevin didn't like me wearing black," I said, not sure I hid the fact I was thoroughly irritated that I had to defend my choice.

*Were people talking about me? Do they think that I'm not devastated because I'm not wearing black?*

My friend, Milly, interrupted my thoughts by handing me a plate of food.

"Sit and eat. You need to get something in your stomach," she said, trying to encourage me. I sat but wasn't at all hungry. I moved the food around on my plate, thinking about eating it, but people began drifting my way to pay last respects and to say goodbye before they departed.

"Let me know if you need anything" was the phrase I was hearing most.

*What could I possibly need other than Kevin back?*

My feet were sore, and I sat back down and saw that someone had cleaned up our table.

*I wasn't hungry anyway.*

My sister sat next to me to say goodbye and put her arms around me.

"I don't want everyone to leave, I want to hear more Kevin stories," I said, not letting up on my embrace.

"I know," she said, rubbing my back. "I'll call you tomorrow," she said.

"When everyone leaves, it will all be real," I said out loud to myself, but she was already walking away and didn't hear me.

She wouldn't have understood anyway.

# Chapter 5

# Kevin the Dog

*October 11, 2015*

Kevin used to refer to Sundays as "Sunday Funday because you get to be lazy all day long." The day after the funeral was not a Sunday Funday. It was the day we had to say goodbye to Kacey—another day with another goodbye.

Of course, we all wished the circumstances were different, but meeting someone who shared a love for my son is what I would call one of the silver linings. Kevin's girlfriend, Kacey, had allowed us to see Kevin through her eyes, giving us glimpses into the last three months of his life.

I didn't want her to leave; she seemed like the only one who could keep him alive a little longer by regaling me with every detail, however mundane, of his day-to-day life. She had brought back all the cards and notes I had sent during the thirteen months he had been in California along with his show tickets, wristbands, t-shirts, cell phone, passport, backpack, and laptop.

We had several one-on-one conversations, sharing stories of Kevin; one of which was that they had recently seen the animated movie *Happy Feet*, which spurred the idea for them to be penguins for the Halloween party they had planned to go to. During that conversation, something had reminded her of a recent photo she had taken of Kevin wearing her sunglasses. She picked up her phone, started scrolling through her photos, softly smiled when she found it, and handed me her phone. He was laughing in the picture, wearing her brow line sunglasses with an uncharacteristically plain green t-shirt.

*Of course, he was laughing.*

I held her phone, enlarging the photo with my fingers so I could go over every detail. I remember thinking I hadn't really noticed how nicely his teeth had come out after a two-year stint in braces. He was holding a straw wrapper in his hands, and upon closer inspection of his fingertips, I could see that he hadn't stopped biting his nails.

He had commented, "I like these sunglasses because they cover my eyebrows as sunglasses should," she told us.

Standing in the kitchen, having our last sips of coffee, we felt her departure looming.

Tom was the one who broke the silence saying, "Can't we keep you?"

I couldn't have picked a better way to express what I was feeling. I wanted more Kevin stories, and she was the only person with new and recent ones.

Her flight back to California was at 8:00 a.m. out of the Boston Logan airport. Tom, Matthew, and I were going into the city for the drop-off and to say goodbye. She, too, had expressed how glad she was to have met Kevin's family and friends and to see where he grew up. It was her first time on the east coast, and she was glad to see his beloved state of New Hampshire—so beloved, in fact, that he tattooed the state on his arm.

When my kids were teenagers, Mike Tyson was all over the media for getting his face tattooed. We had talked about tattoos and putting something permanent on our bodies. At the time, I was trying to use it as an example of why not to get one.

Flashforward to my forty-eighth birthday when Kevin flew home to surprise me. He knew I would be so focused on how thoughtful the surprise visit was that I wouldn't be completely on my guard.

He told me before he showed me, and when he saw the disappointment on my face, he quickly lifted his shirt sleeve exposing the tattoo which was the outline of the state of New Hampshire. Inside the outline was the state's official motto, "Live Free or Die," written in the center.

Before I could say a word, he interjected. "Mom, I was homesick. When anybody asks me where I'm from, I always say 'New Hampshire for *damn* sure.' It's my line."

The truth was when I saw that tattoo was of his home state and heard he was homesick, I melted. I was sad that he was sad, but it also felt good to know he had missed being home; and now he was home, and that was all that mattered to me.

"I like it," I said and hugged him tightly.

Knowing I wasn't upset, he was able to focus on Manny who had been trying to get Kevin's attention by prancing around with a toy in his mouth. He knelt on the floor and petted Manny, which effectively ended the tattoo discussion.

It was Columbus Day weekend, but at 6:00 a.m. on Sunday, there wasn't any traffic. Tom had connected Kevin's iPod so we could play his music through the car's speakers on the way to the airport. We all sat quietly during the ride, Matthew and Kacey in the backseat, listening to the music and feeling lost in our own thoughts, completely unsure of what else to say to each other because no words could really describe what each of us was going through.

I was staring out the window, noticing nothing but how the sun was shining and how wrong that seemed. I tried to listen to some of the lyrics playing, hoping to hear some hidden message from Kevin. I still hadn't gotten any message from him to let me know he was okay.

When the Grateful Dead's "Ripple" started playing, I listened, hoping for a message in the lyrics. I thought of what Matthew said to Kevin in the eulogy "... your ripple has been set into motion." I did not yet know the impact that those words would eventually have on me.

*Was he letting me know he had to go alone? Was that my sign? Would a sign take this much guesswork?*

We arrived at terminal B departures at Logan and pulled up to the curb. We got out of the car and waited while Tom pulled her luggage from the trunk and placed it at her feet. "Goodbye, Kacey from Cali," he said as he bent over to hug her.

"Bye, Tom. Thank you," she said, wiping tears.

She turned to me. "Thank you for everything, Susan." We leaned in for a hug. "Bye, honey. Text me when you land, please," I said.

"I will," she said and faced Matthew who had stepped forward for his turn.

She gave me a small wave and turned toward the sliding doors. I watched her back disappear into the airport, feeling my chest tighten. My last lifeline to Kevin was now gone.

Driving home from the airport, panic started setting in. There was nothing pressing left *to do*, and I still hadn't received any sign yet. I wasn't sure what I was expecting, but I was pretty sure the line from "Ripple" wasn't it. I was trying to pay attention, but my grief was so heavy.

I didn't have any expectations, at least not of how the sign would arrive or what it would look like. I had just assumed Kevin would make sure that I knew it was from him and that he was okay. I assumed I would just know.

*Could I have missed it?*

When we arrived home, Matthew went back to bed. His world was also shattered, and I was at a loss of how to help him. Leaning against the kitchen counter for support, I shared with Tom that I had asked Kevin for a sign.

"The last thing I said to Kev before they closed the casket was to please give me a sign to let me know he's okay, but I've not heard from him."

I wanted Tom to say something comforting, but he just sighed.

"What are we supposed to do now?" We had been *doing* for eight straight days, and there was nothing left to do.

Tom looked at me with a blank stare. "I don't know."

Every time I allowed myself to think about the future, even if it was just the next day, I panicked.

*How do you go on after your child dies?*

There were no directions for this. There was no plan.

All of it was too big and scary to think about.

I left the kitchen to grab my hiking shoes and came back to find Tom slumped in a chair at the kitchen table with his face in his hands.

"Let's take the dogs for a walk," I suggested.

He nodded without argument or any other suggestion. For the last week, he had been attending to the business side of Kevin's death, the arrangements that needed to be taken care of. He, too, was at a loss for what to do next. Time would be forever marked as *before and after* Kevin died, and with the funeral now over, this somehow felt like our first official day in L.A.K.—life after Kevin. I didn't have any directions as to how to be in the world. Nothing would ever be the same.

Getting out in nature with my dogs had always been my go-to before Kevin died, so maybe this was something to hold onto. But even a walk in the woods didn't seem normal anymore, and my approach with Manny and Tripp had already changed. Before Kevin died, I would not let Manny and Tripp greet other dogs in the woods. I had many experiences over the years where people said their dog was friendly only for their dog to start growling with hackles up. Before Kevin died, I would say hello, but I would not stop to talk to people, especially those with dogs.

On this day, Tom and I decided we were going to have Kevin's attitude and be more friendly. On this day, we were going to talk to people on the trails. On this day, we attempted to bring Kevin's spirit as close to us as we could.

* * *

We pulled into the parking lot of the local conservation area in our town three miles from my house. I opened the tailgate of my truck, grabbed two leashes, and let the dogs out of their crates. It felt surreal to be in a familiar place, yet everything felt different. The entrance to the dirt parking lot was framed with oaks and pine trees. I was surprised to see several cars there until I remembered it was Columbus Day weekend.

The fall foliage was a few weeks away from the peak. It was unseasonably warm with the sun shining and temperatures in the 70s. The dogs knew where they were, and as soon as they were on the trail, they got busy catching up on the smells they'd missed over the past couple of weeks. I didn't have much energy and was glad I picked a trail that was wide and flat.

No matter how much time we had spent training, almost every day would include time walking in the woods where they could just be dogs. I was never one to go to a gym to work out. For me, hiking in the woods surrounded by beauty and the extra oxygen given off by the trees had always left me feeling at peace.

Manny was so excited to be on familiar turf he dropped on his side and had a luxurious roll on his back with his hind legs moving in the air like he was riding an imaginary bike. Seeing him enjoy himself so thoroughly had taken me out of my head and into the moment where, for a few seconds, everything was right again. When he was done, he flipped on his side, stood up, and completed the process with a good shake.

It was the shake that snapped me back into my misery. This was my *new normal*.

Suddenly, the woods were no longer a place of refuge to ease the day's problems. Kevin's death had been too much. The woods had lost their magic.

Tom and I continued our walk mostly in silence. We watched the dogs switch their attention back and forth from sniffing the trail to making sure we were still there. A woman up ahead had just turned onto our trail coming from the opposite direction. She saw the dogs, and a smile came across her face, which meant she might be open to greet them. I called them to me and slipped the leashes over their heads, pausing on the trail in case the woman wanted to say hello. I gave Manny a plastic toy to hold in his mouth while we waited.

Manny, more than any dog I've ever had, loved to greet people, but being greeted by two excited dogs can be a little much. I had brought only one toy, and I knew Tripp would have taken it from him, which would have deflated Manny's greeting process. I had Tripp sit next to me while Manny worked his charm. Carrying anything in his mouth made Manny excited, which would make him whine or *talk* (as I like to call it). The golden retriever part of him loved to *show* the person he was greeting what he had in his mouth.

"What beautiful dogs. May I pet them?" the woman asked.

"He would love that," I said, managing a small smile.

By this time, Manny was pacing in front of her, whining, with the toy in his mouth. She reached down to take it from him, naturally thinking he wanted her to throw it or play tug.

"He doesn't want you to throw it. He's just showing it to you. He'll be super happy if you just tell him how awesome you think it is," I said.

He had done this talking with a toy in his mouth since puppyhood. In the past, when a person would take his toy, his body would immediately stop wagging, and he would walk away with his head down. If there was such a thing as a dog slouching, that would be him. She followed my instructions perfectly by putting her hands on her knees and bending toward him saying, "What do you have there, Manny?" This made him whine even louder, and he started moving his body side-to-side in what I call a full-body wag.

"What a happy boy," she said, looking up at us, then glancing over to Tripp. Tripp took her direct eye contact as an invitation to take a few steps forward and say hello. Manny dropped the toy and walked back to me for some consolation petting while Tripp picked up the greeting where Manny left off.

When his greeting started to wane, she stood up and said, "Enjoy this beautiful day," which snapped me out of the moment and back to Kevin.

"Same to you," I said, and we walked in opposite directions. I stopped a few paces later to take the leashes back off the dogs to let them roam freely again.

When she was out of earshot, I said, "We are doing a good job," and looked at Tom. "Kev would be happy we are out and talking to people."

"I agree," he said.

We had done the trail loop and were on the last thirty yards that led back to the parking lot when a family who had just approached the trail entrance started walking toward us—a mother, grandmother, a young boy, and a girl with a *very* excited white and tan boxer mix. The dog was at the end of his leash, pulling the mother toward us, acting more like a sled dog.

Based on my experience with excited dogs, I started to anticipate a problem but then reminded myself that we were trying to be open like Kevin. The dog was wagging frantically like he was greeting old friends and seemingly excited, not aggressive. Tom and I stopped once more so I could slip the leashes back over their heads before the family reached us.

The three dogs were intrigued with each other, tails wagging, taking turns sniffing and being sniffed. Tom and the mother were making small talk while I kept my eye on the dogs, untangling leashes and making sure their behavior didn't take a turn. The grandmother and two kids were standing off to the side of the trail letting the dogs have their greeting.

The Boxer mix went down on his elbows, hoisting his butt up in the air to signal a game of chase, which was the natural end to the conversation. A pack of three excited dogs zipping around six people was not a good idea. I petted my leg for Manny and Tripp to come close to me, and we said goodbye to the family.

We had just turned to leave when we heard the mother say, "Let's go, Kevin."

Tom and I stopped in our tracks just hearing his name. We both turned around expecting her to be looking at her son, but *she was looking at her dog.* The dog was at the end of his leash ignoring her, and completely focused on us.

"Come on Kev," she said.

We were standing just a few feet away with our mouths agape, looking at this dog who didn't want to leave us.

*Oh my God. This is my sign.*

Later, I would think of all the things that had to line up to create this perfect moment of connection. Like the fact I chose that particular trail when I have access to over eighty-five miles of local trails to choose from. Had we not opted to take Kevin's friendly demeanor with us and talk to people we saw, we would have passed right by the family and never known that dog's name was Kevin. We also would have passed by the lady who greeted Manny and Tripp, which would have had us done with our walk sooner, and we would have missed the family's arrival altogether.

I didn't or couldn't move or speak for fear of breaking the moment.

I glanced back to the mother "Your dog's name is Kevin??" I said half asking and half stating in disbelief.

"Yes, he's a rescue," she said, implying he came with the unusual dog name.

I pulled out a wad of damp tissues from my pocket and looked at Tom who stood wide-eyed and stunned. When we didn't reply, she pulled on Kevin the Dog's leash who was still uninterested in moving away from us.

Tom looked at me and asked, "Should I tell her?"

"Yes!" I said and gestured with my arm to catch up to her.

I put the dogs on a down-stay so Tom could talk with her without interruption and to give me a moment to absorb the magnitude of what was happening.

I couldn't take my eyes off of Kevin the Dog who was looking at me just as intently while Tom, who was twenty feet away, told the mother that our son Kevin's funeral was yesterday. She covered her mouth and hugged Tom. I knelt in front of Manny and Tripp and patted my leg. They sat up next to me, and I wrapped my arms around their bodies. The three of us huddled together with my face buried in the fur between them. I kissed both dogs and wiped fresh tears on their coats, and one of them gently licked my ear in response.

"Thank you," I said, whispering into their soft ears my gratitude for their part in our receiving this miracle.

Tom finished and came back over to us, and I stood up. "Did that just happen?" I asked.

"I know," he said, marveling. "That was crazy. I mean who the hell names their dog Kevin?!"

We stood in amazement as the family went around the bend and out of sight. Walking back to the truck I felt a little lighter. I lifted the dogs into the truck and closed the door. What was I feeling? A flutter of excitement? Hope?

On the way home, Tom and I discussed how perfectly in character that was for Kevin. My answer was delivered loud and clear.

*I'm here, I'm okay, and you are capable of smiling in your darkest hour.*

When we got home, I let the dogs out in our fenced patio area and went straight to my computer. My screen lit up, and I excitedly started typing out an email to Kacey, recounting the Kevin the Dog sign. She had also asked Kevin for a sign, and I wanted to let her know it was really possible to get one. I knew she would agree that his sign and delivery were perfect.

I checked my email the next morning to read that Kacey received her sign. too ...

*Dear Susan & Tom,*

*Thank you for that story! Very reassuring, I'm happy Kev seems at peace and well. It's comforting to know he's watching over us all. I too have been feeling anxious about not sensing his presence ...*

*My mom texted me while I was in NH and she said, "I asked God to allow Kev to send you a message so if you see a butterfly or hummingbird or penguin, it may be Kev."*

*I thought it was sweet of her but remember thinking to myself, that if a butterfly would appear it wouldn't mean it was Kev. At least not to me. And while I love humming-birds, they too are not how Kev would appear for me. I also remember thinking; Kev would come as a penguin but where the hell would I encounter a sign like that?*

*Well ... on my first flight back, I boarded and was sitting by the window. A woman asked me if I could switch places with her, I agreed.*

*I switched and was in my new seat for less than a minute when the girl next to me asked "Would you mind switching again so that I may sit next to my young daughter?" I agreed once more.*

*As soon as I got comfortable in my new seat, I noticed the young girl was hugging what else ... but a penguin stuffed animal. Tears rolled for me as I smiled and silently said hi to Kev. The penguin seemed to stare at me for nearly the entire flight ... Love to you guys.*

*Chat with you soon,*
*Kacey from Cali*

Tom, who had been hopeful but skeptical about signs, was the one who pointed out the fact that these two events happened within a couple of hours of each other. I was grateful that Kevin had chosen to give two humorous signs that were so unmistakably aligned with his personality that even Tom couldn't deny they were from Kevin.

Kevin's ripple had been set into motion.

## Chapter 6

# Endings and Beginnings

*December 2015*

Having the Kevin the Dog story in writing allowed me to reread and relive the moment fifty times the week it happened, each time etching another detail into my memory. It was the first sign I've ever had, and it opened me up to the idea that connecting with Kevin was still possible. Ironically, the lift I felt from that glorious sign lasted mere days because I was waiting for the next one to happen. Plus, my grief in those early months was deafening and blinding all at once, making it hard at times to know if I was missing signs or whether I had only imagined that first one despite it being written down and despite Tom having been there, too.

And there was the steep learning curve of what my life was now supposed to be like in the thick of grief. I couldn't begin to imagine life on the other side of it—if there even was one. I wasn't certain of anything other than the pain and loss I was enduring and that the only comfort and safety I felt was with Tom, Manny, and Tripp and being at home.

Learning how to be alongside my grief when I was safely in my home was one thing, but being out in public, exposed to daily life that continued as if nothing happened, was entirely different. I had yet to learn how to navigate this "new normal."

Matthew had gone back to his apartment in Montreal at the beginning of November, and Tom was back going to the office. Most of his colleagues knew about Kevin, but part of Tom's job was meeting with customers for business dinners. He shared with me how, when meeting someone for the first time, especially over dinner, the conversation almost always landed on the topic of kids. "It's as easy as talking about the weather ... usually" he had said. He shared a cringe-worthy moment when small talk had shifted in that direction.

"I had dinner tonight with co-workers and some people I hadn't met before. Halfway through the meal, one of them asked me if I had any kids," Tom said as he slipped into bed.

I propped my elbow onto my pillow to face him. "What did you say?"

"I told him. He was obviously horrified and said he was sorry. It fucking sucked."

When he offered nothing else, I laid back down, each of us on our own side of the bed, quiet in our own thoughts.

*Yes, it does.*

The places I went to on a regular basis were to the grocery store and to the small veterinary practice where I worked. Everyone I worked with already knew about Kevin, but I also understood the pain of telling people outside of my office that my son died. You never knew when it was going to happen, but you could always count on the reaction.

When going out in public, the goal was always the same, which was to try not to fall apart. Grocery shopping proved to be more challenging than I anticipated. The first time I opted to go, I made some flimsy plan of not going down the snack aisle with all the chips. I knew that might be a trigger because Kevin loved salty snacks. When he was living with us, I had a secret place where I'd hide the Pringles and Smartfood popcorn because if he saw them in the cabinet, he wouldn't have just a few; he'd eat the whole bag. Kevin couldn't do anything just a little bit when he loved something.

The plan to avoid the snack aisles had a poor success rate. I'd start pushing my shopping cart down the dairy aisle and be okay, but the next aisle was the pasta aisle that had Kraft macaroni and cheese. My memory would taunt me by bringing up the image of ten-year-old Kevin standing in front of the blue and gold boxes strategically positioned at a kid's eye level. "Mom! They have Rugrats mac and cheese!!" he'd say, somehow thinking I'd be as excited as he was upon his discovery.

When I felt the emotion rising, I'd push it down by pushing past the memory with my carriage, turning into the next aisle, hoping it would stay down. One day, I had gone into the grocery store just to get a few things in the produce section.

Normally, I entered on the other side of the store, but on this day, I entered on the side near the frozen food, grabbed a basket, and started walking. As I passed the freezer doors, I saw popsicles and slowed, stopping at the ice cream doors.

*This isn't going to end well, Susan. Keep walking. Why are you torturing yourself?*

Seeing the pints of chocolate chip cookie dough made my heart start to pound, knowing the lead blanket was coming.

My chest hurt as my grief crawled around my shoulders, gripping me tight. I put the basket down right where I was standing and hurried out of the store. It didn't even matter to me that some poor store clerk was going to have to put the contents away. I would never have done that in the past, but in the past, Kevin was alive. I needed to get home.

. . .

Going to work was a different story. I went back to my role as a receptionist at the veterinary hospital in an attempt to get back into some familiarity. I thought having some part of my old life back or old routine would bring comfort or the ability to focus on something other than being lost inside my grief. But nothing from my old life felt the same.

Part of my job as a receptionist was to field phone calls, book appointments, answer client questions, cash out clients, and take messages for the doctors. A particularly hard part of my job was also to take calls from teary clients who were coming to terms with saying goodbye to a member of their family of which I could relate 100%.

It was a conversation I had many times with clients in the past, and even though they were not my pets, these conversations were now even harder. There was nothing that didn't somehow compare or relate to my current grief. It was like I had put on a pair of glasses, and they were only capable of seeing the world through the lens of grief. I had to try and keep my feelings in check while at work just on normal days, but after those particular phone calls, I'd be slipping into the bathroom to break down in private. I couldn't just drop what I was doing and escape to my home.

*Don't fall apart Susan. Compartmentalize. Wait until you get home before you cry. It makes people uncomfortable when you cry in front of them. They want you to feel better.*

Having worked at the hospital for several years, I had gotten to know many of the clients and their pets. There was one client, Betty, who came in often with her tiny dog, Pebbles. Pebbles had diabetes and was Betty's constant companion. Betty normally came to appointments with her adult daughter, but one day neither had shown up for the dog's insulin check. It was unusual for them to miss an appointment without notifying us. I dialed her phone number with trepidation hoping that something hadn't happened. We hadn't received anything overnight from any of the ER veterinary hospitals.

I heard Betty's phone ring once, then it went right to voicemail.

"Hello. This is Susan at the veterinary hospital. Please give us a call back so we can reschedule the appointment for Pebbles' insulin follow-up. Please call us at your earliest convenience."

She never called back.

A few days later Betty walked into the clinic cradling four-pound Pebbles, her fawn-colored Chihuahua, like a baby. I could tell by how Betty hung her head something was very wrong. She was normally friendly and chatty, but as she walked toward the front desk, I thought she might stumble. The blonde curls of her hair that were normally tamed into a single braid, were left to do as they wished, which made her look even more disheveled.

When she looked up at me, her normally bright blue eyes were puffy and red-rimmed. She looked like she hadn't slept in days. As soon as she saw me, she started to apologize for missing her appointment but stopped and suddenly burst into tears.

"I'm so sorry ..." she blurted out, wiping her cheeks with a Kleenex. She was looking directly at Pebbles. "I can't have anything happen to her ..."

"What's wrong? What happened to her?" I asked.

On hearing our conversation, my coworker, Jenny, abruptly got up and started to rush to get one of the doctors.

Realizing our confusion, she tried to stop Jenny. "No, no, no," she said, waving her hand for her to stop.

Jenny went back to her desk to answer the phone that just started ringing.

I got up from my chair and came from around the desk. I took Betty's hand and walked her to a chair in the waiting room. It was the doctor's lunch hour, so thankfully the waiting room was empty, giving us some privacy. We sat down, and she put her face in her free hand still holding the tiny Chihuahua on her lap and started to sob. I waited for her to compose herself enough to speak.

"My daughter ...," she started. And I felt it.

She didn't have to say anymore. I just knew.

"My daughter died ... a heroin overdose," she said, wiping her eyes with the back of her free hand.

I couldn't speak for fear I'd lose my composure. She slowly looked up and met my eyes that had fresh tears welling. I was witnessing my worst nightmare—a mother who had lost a child due to overdose and the horror of knowing she had been powerless to prevent it.

"I'm so sorry," I whispered. "I also know the pain of losing a child. My son died a couple months ago."

"What happened to him?" she asked.

"We don't know yet. The toxicology report hasn't come back yet."

"I'm so sorry for you as well."

She reached for my hand, and we sat for a moment in silence, grieving for our losses and each other. At that moment, I wished there was a magic wall that would go up around us to give us some privacy, but there was none. We needed some time to bottle up the pain that had spilled out and tuck it away until we got home or at least to our car.

The door opened and slammed shut, startling Betty and me and interrupting our quiet, delicate conversation. The man who came in looked at us briefly, then started to talk to Jenny behind the desk. It was just the thing to jar us both back into our reality—sitting there in the waiting room under the world's observation. Betty released my hands and adjusted the dog in her lap.

"I don't know what I'd do without her," she sniffed and lifted Pebbles to her face, kissing her tiny head.

I knew exactly what she meant.

Pebbles may have been only four pounds, but she was Betty's lifeline, just like Manny and Tripp were for me. I was still their mother; they still needed me. I knew how to take care of them, and they knew how to take care of me. I couldn't imagine if either of them suddenly had a health crisis.

"Let's get you an appointment to check her insulin so we don't have to worry about that, okay?" I said, trying to lift the mood a bit.

"Yes. Good idea," she said, and we both got up. I walked back to my computer behind the desk.

I gave her a card with her appointment written down and told her I'd call her home phone and leave a message to remind her just in case she misplaced the reminder card.

"Thank you," she said, giving me a sympathetic look. I stayed in my chair knowing that if I came around to hug her, that would be the end of my composure. I nodded, blew her a kiss, and gave a small wave goodbye. Jenny was on the phone, and when I looked down at mine, I saw two people were on hold.

I took a deep breath, picked up the receiver, and pressed the hold button, mustering the cheeriest voice I could manage. "Hello. This is Susan. How can I help you?"

* * *

In addition to avoiding going most places outside the house, I was also avoiding finalizing some of the remaining administrative details of the "business of death" like closing Kevin's bank account. I knew I had to do it, but I hated the idea of having to speak to someone or, worse yet, going and seeing them in-person.

I had already called his bank at least once, and the account manager told me that since I was not a joint member on the account, they required me to come in-person. So now I had to call to make that appointment.

I picked up the phone and called the bank.

"Hello. I'd like to make an appointment to close an account."

"Okay. I will transfer you over to the account manager. Hold, please."

"Sure."

"Hello. This is Karen. How can I help you?"

"Hi, Karen. I need to close my son's bank account. He ... um, died."

"Okay. What was his name?"

"His name *is* Kevin Lynch"

*I'm not ready to use his name in the past tense.*

"Okay. So you need to bring in a copy of the death certificate and your driver's license." Her voice had sounded somewhat muffled like the mouthpiece was in her neck.

"Excuse me?" I said, wanting to make sure I heard her correctly.

"Oh sorry," she said too loudly, apparently, having adjusted the mouthpiece. "A death certificate," she repeated, saying the word "death" with extra emphasis.

*No condolences?*

"Yes, I have one." I was still confused as to how we skipped over acknowledgment and got right to the paperwork.

"I can see you tomorrow at 2:00 p.m. Please make sure it is a *certified* copy of the death certificate. We don't accept photocopies. It needs to have a raised seal on it."

*You don't accept photocopies?? What happened to "I'm sorry for your loss"?*

"Yes, it has a seal," I said, swallowing hard.

"Okay. When we have that, we will freeze the account and get the paperwork going."

"Okay," I said, feeling defeated.

"Great. See you tomorrow afternoon at 2:00. Have a great day!" she said in a cheerful voice, obviously scripted.

*I just told her I needed to close my son's bank account, not open one. Closing his account feels like more of his life is being erased ... Did she really just say "Have a great day"?*

I hung up and put my cell phone down.

*Freeze the account.*

It all sounded so final.

●  ●  ●

The next day at 2:00 I opened the door of the bank and walked in. This had been his bank for years, and I remembered the last time I was here.

It was a few years before he died when he was in his early twenties. He was heading to work and had asked me if I would deposit one of his work checks for him. I gave the teller his account number and slid the signed check toward her. She typed in the information, pulling up his account, and looked up at me with a big smile "You're Kevin's mother?!"

"Yes." I felt a pang of nervousness.

"Oh my God. We love him. He is so funny!" She promptly reached under the counter for her phone. She swiped the screen with her finger and turned her phone to show me a photo she had taken of him on Halloween. He had come in to deposit his check on his way into Boston for a Halloween party dressed as the Chinese philosopher Confucius.

I couldn't remember if the woman in front of me was the same bank teller. I glided my thumb over the laminated picture of him in my pocket and thought about pulling it out to show her. But when she looked up at me, I chickened out.

"Hi. My name is Susan Lynch. I have an appointment with Karen at 2:00."

"Oh sure. I will let her know you are here. Just a moment." She picked up the phone to let her know of my arrival, then hung up again.

"She is in the second door on the right."

"Okay. Thank you," I said, rubbing the laminated photo a second time. I followed the teller's instructions and walked to the second door on the right.

Karen's door was open, but she was completely immersed in what she was doing at her computer, unaware of me standing on the threshold of her office door. She wore a canary yellow blazer that looked a little too big and bordered on garish over a black blouse. She looked like either a large bird or a hornet.

"Karen?" I said quietly knowing better than to startle a hornet. "Yes?" she said abruptly and looked up.

"I'm Susan Lynch. I have an appointment with you to close my son's account."

"Oh yes. Right." I couldn't tell if she was annoyed that I disrupted her or if that was her everyday attitude. "Come in and have a seat," she said, gesturing toward the metal chair.

I took it upon myself to close the door for privacy and sat down, suddenly feeling chilly. I kept my coat on. Her desk was oversized, but she managed to fill most of the space. To her left was an eight-inch stack of manilla files that looked like a to-do pile. The walls of her office were painted a neutral beige with a picture of a certificate of some kind on the wall. There was a green plant on a stand in the corner that was drooping as if it was in desperate need of water.

"Did you bring a *certified* death certificate?" she said, emphasizing the word "certified."

"Yes," I said and passed it to her.

"And your license please," she said flatly as she examined the certificate.

I reached down to my purse and opened my wallet and pulled out my ID.

"I need to make a copy of it."

"Okay."

She placed it in the scanner and pushed the button. The copier needed a few seconds to warm up, and there was an awkward silence while she waited for it to spit out the piece of paper.

She handed it back to me, turned to her computer, and started tapping away on her keyboard.

"Okay. We've frozen the account, and I just sent the information to corporate headquarters. Give us two weeks to be safe to come back in for the check."

"Should I make an appointment?"

"No need. I'm here on Fridays; and all you have to do is sign a form, and I'll give you the check."

"Okay. Thank you."

She gave her canned reply. "Have a great day!"

I forced a smile and said nothing. I couldn't think of anything polite to say.

Two weeks later, I walked back into the bank and over to the same teller so she could alert Karen, the very busy account manager.

"Hi. I am here to see Karen."

"Okay. Do you have an appointment?"

"I do not. I am just here to pick up a check."

"Okay. Let me see if she's in her office."

The teller picked up the phone, pushed a couple buttons, and mumbled something into the phone before hanging up.

"Yes, she's here. Her office is the second door on the right." She pointed back down the hall.

I walked over to her office and knocked.

"Hi, Karen. My name is Susan Lynch. I was here a couple of weeks ago to close my son's …"

"Oh yes," she interrupted, suddenly remembering me and sounding annoyed and started rummaging through the pile of papers on her desk.

*It's not just me. This is her everyday annoyed voice.*

"Hmmm. I just need to get the paperwork for you to sign, but I am not seeing it here," she mumbled, moving through the pile of files faster.

After a minute of unsuccessful shuffling of papers, she huffed, completely exasperated, putting both palms on her desk to try and calm herself. She looked directly at me and said, "I have so many bereavement files it's like my second job. Let me check the other office. I'll be right back."

She got up and left the office, leaving me alone, feeling as if I was being a burden, another to-do item in her pile. My knee-jerk reaction was to apologize, but I didn't. I got angry.

*Why is it that ever since I've been dealing with this woman, she has completely ignored WHY I'm even here?*

I sat in an uncomfortable chair with my arms around my waist in an attempt to console myself. I started to rock, focusing on the light snow that was falling just outside her office window. It was starting to stick, hiding the dirtier snow underneath. I closed my eyes and took a deep breath, trying to calm the anger that was starting to make me stiffen.

*Shouldn't every death get an "I'm sorry for your loss"?*

Karen briskly walked back into her office as if she were trying to make up for the lost time she had spent looking for his paperwork. She took out a document and spun it around, offering me a pen, indicating she needed my signature.

"I just need to see your license again," she said a bit more cheerfully, regaining her composure.

Her desk was positioned so she sat with her back to a large picture window. It struck me how much beauty and peace were just beyond her, her stack of files, and my uncomfortable chair. I reached for the pen and signed my name, officially closing Kevin's account. She straightened out the papers, looked up at me with a tight smile, and passed me the check.

"Have a great day," she said holding the fake smile and slightly tipping her head to the side.

This time I had fully expected her response, acting as if she were handing me a college loan check to put toward Kevin's future. I stood up and forced a smile.

"Thank you," I said and walked out of her office, trying to keep my head up, trying to pretend I didn't feel completely out of place anywhere other than at home or in the woods with my dogs.

I opened the door and walked outside, stepping into what looked like a scene in a snow globe. Drawing in a deep breath of the cold air, I reached for my keys and walked to my car, thinking of a plan to attempt to release the stickiness of my feelings.

I drove directly home, pulled my car into the garage, and closed the door behind. The snow was starting to pile up, and it was looking like we might have a white Christmas after all. The dogs greeted me as I walked into the kitchen, sniffing my legs in an attempt to find out where I'd been.

"Tripp, you don't wanna inhale any of Karen's energy." He sneezed in response. "Good you blew it out."

The dogs followed me into the sunroom. As I laid down on the couch, they each chose a spot on the floor next to me. Watching the snowflakes fall had a kind of hypnotic effect, relaxing my mind and body from the unpleasantness of the bank. I fell asleep for about an hour and woke up to Manny licking my hands.

"Hey, Manny," I said, stretching out one arm as the other rubbed his ear.

I sat up and looked out the window to see it was still snowing, and my eyes landed on the spot in the room where we normally set up the Christmas tree. I felt the sudden urge to set up the tree for Kevin. It felt like a nudge from him, and I went with it.

When the kids were little, we used to cut down our tree until we realized Kevin's asthma worsened around Christmastime. We bought a fake one years ago, and although it wasn't the same, it was effective in reducing his discomfort.

"Okay, Kev. You win. I'm gonna set up the tree."

I got up and moved the couch over, making more space. I walked up the attic stairs and grabbed the long box that had the tree in it. I carried it down and laid it on the sunroom floor, attracting the dog's attention. They began inspecting the prickly contents. The tree was in three pieces that took less than one minute to assemble but fifteen minutes to fluff up the flattened branches.

"How's that, Kev? I think it looks good."

When Matthew went to college in Canada, it was Kevin and me who set up the tree each Christmas. I would unravel the lights, and when they were all untangled, Kevin and I would stand on either side of the tree each making sure our sides were even.

When the tree was all set up and in position, I went back up into the attic to get the box of lights and the box marked "Christmas ornaments." This year, I would have to continuously walk around the tree instead of passing them to Kevin.

"How am I doing, Kev? Does it look even?"

By the time the lights were strung, it was dark outside, and the twinkling gave a mellow glow to the room. Opening the box of ornaments, I started carefully unwrapping the bubble wrap around the delicate ones, knowing they were handmade from when the boys were in preschool and elementary school. There were strings of spray-painted macaroni, a first-grade school photo in a blue star frame, a Rudolph face made of popsicle sticks and pipe cleaners complete with a yarn scarf. I put them all in prominent spots, high enough on the tree where the dogs' noses couldn't reach, and stood looking at all the precious memories represented in front of me. It seemed like we were missing some ornaments and thought I should take another look in the attic. I looked at Manny and Tripp. "I'll be right back."

Rummaging through the boxes in the attic, I continued to have a strong feeling we were missing something. When I came across a box marked "Christmas Wrapping Paper," I knew it wasn't a logical one to check, but I opened it anyway. There, sitting right on top of the rolls of wrapping paper, was a lone Christmas ornament. The ornament was a black and white penguin wearing red and white earmuffs. He was standing on a cloud rimmed in white glitter with a red jingle bell hanging from the bottom. Written on the cloud was "Merry Christmas, Mom!" I couldn't move. I sat staring at the penguin smiling and waving hello with its flipper.

*Kevin gave me this ornament when he was about thirteen years old.*

Suddenly, I realized Kevin had given me all the urges to find it.

*Put up the Christmas tree. Talk to him.*

*Check the attic once more.*

I followed those urges like little breadcrumbs that led me to the wrapping paper box. I was *feeling* him keeping our conversation going with nudges.

Sitting on the cold floor in the attic, I held the ornament close to my chest and cried bittersweet tears. He found a way to wish me a Merry Christmas.

"Thank you, Kev. Merry Christmas. I love you so much," I whispered.

I came down from the attic and brought the penguin over to the Christmas tree and hung it in the front.

Turning to the dogs, I said, "Do you guys sense Kevin, too? He's here. He just wished me a Merry Christmas. I know it sounds strange, but it just happened!"

Manny responded by bringing me his fleece ball. I wasn't sure if that was his way of agreeing with me or if he thought I needed some extra love and attention. I turned back to the tree and marveled at the waving penguin staring back at me.

This was my second sign from Kevin, and although I couldn't physically see him, I *felt* him and knew this was his way to reach out to us. But I was already learning quickly that a sign from Kevin was both fleeting and addicting—I treasured it when it happened, but it never lasted as long as I wanted; and it always left me longing for another. I would do what I could to learn the intricacies of our new relationship with him in spirit; I just had no idea where to begin.

The penguin sign was a lift, but the lift was brief. Christmas was just around the corner, and I was dreading it. Thanksgiving had come and gone, painfully, with a lot of crying, and I wasn't anticipating this holiday to be any better. I told Tom and Matthew that I wasn't up for handling gifts the way we had done in the past. I didn't want to wrap presents nor did I want to exchange gifts on Christmas morning by the tree. Opening gifts alongside the tree was something the four of us did together, and it was just too painful without Kevin. Instead, I unceremoniously handed out unwrapped gifts throughout the month of December.

Normally, every Christmas Eve we go to Tom's brother's, and we host Christmas Day dinner. Tom's approach to the holidays was the opposite of mine—he wanted to keep as much the same as possible. I'd have preferred to skip both of them, but I agreed to host Christmas dinner at our house. At least I could slip into Kevin's room for privacy if I needed to.

Of the two events, Christmas Eve was the one I was dreading the most. I mostly didn't want to leave my house, and every family member who went on the Costa Rica trip would be there except for Kevin. I was not at all comfortable being around people, even family, especially for such a family-based holiday like Christmas Eve, but I ended up going to support Tom. He too was in deep pain, and by doing something that he wanted, I felt like I was helping him with his grief.

On Christmas Eve, the three of us walked into my brother's-in-law house. My sister-in-law walked over to me and gave me a hug.

"I'm so glad you guys are here," she said into my ear.

I didn't trust myself to speak for fear I'd start crying, so I responded with a nod and a tight smile.

Walking from the foyer, the first thing my eyes landed on was the couch right off their kitchen. The couch that Tom, Matthew, Kevin, and I sat on with our arms linked and had our photo taken last Christmas Eve.

I forced myself to look away, but reminders were everywhere.

The cousins were huddled around the kitchen island, snacking just like they did when we were in Costa Rica—when Kevin was alive. When Kevin was alive, he'd be joking with Matthew and the cousins, and they'd all be laughing. He'd be asking them how their soccer team was doing this year or what their favorite gymnastics event was. When we were in Costa Rica, he had hung out at the pool with the cousins, eating quesadillas. But that was then, and he wasn't here now.

Not hearing him laughing made my cheeks suddenly wet and a lump the size of a walnut swelled in my throat. As always, when outside of my home, I was trying to keep my composure, but the memories were too fresh.

I didn't want to be a spectacle, so I went into the opposite room to quietly fall apart. It was too painful to see all the cousins scattered around the back and arms of the couch to listen to my father-in-law read *The Night Before Christmas* while their parents snapped keepsake photos.

I could hear the muffled voices of my family trying to keep things as normal as possible for the kids' sake, but I couldn't witness it. It was too painful to see Christmas happen without Kevin. For the rest of the evening, I stayed in the opposite room, wanting to be alone. Tom and other family members periodically came in to check on me and ask if I wanted anything, but all I wanted was Kevin back and to go home.

*Chapter 7*

# Following Their Lead

*January 2016*

My grief was so heavy those first few months, I was unable to handle anything other than "the now." I tried to focus on just one day, one moment at a time. The small things suddenly were the big things—remembering to wash my hair, making a grocery list, returning a phone call.

As grief stricken as I was, the one thing I tried not to skip was taking the dogs for our daily walk, though even that wasn't the same. Before Kevin died, I was able to read Manny's and Tripp's behavior, able to anticipate what was coming next and respond quickly. Now my brain was so clouded with grief my processing ability was in slow motion, making walks in the woods more like being in a trance, some kind of walking meditation. Watching them explore what caught their attention was somehow hypnotic—Manny pausing to watch a late-in-the-season butterfly skittering in the air or Tripp's nose meticulously sniffing up and down the length of a fern, collecting the scent details of the dog that was there before him. I didn't know it at the time, but learning how to pause when the Universe sent along something that snagged my attention would be the very beginning of how I would learn to connect with Kevin.

Manny and Tripp continued their vigilance on our walks, pausing to make sure I was still with them, occasionally trotting back to me for a check-in and a quick pat on the head before going back to their exploration. At home, they intuitively were able to tell when I needed them next to me for extra emotional support, and if I didn't, they'd just lay close by. When I stood, they'd lift their heads up, watching me as if I were an elderly person who might fall.

When we weren't on walks, we were in one of two other places. At the computer or in Kevin's room. If I was at the computer, I was rereading Kevin the Dog or researching parent grief, trying to figure out how to do it right.

Most articles had the similar theme of everyone grieves differently, that there are no rules, no linear progression, and no timetable. I hated that. I hated it all. It was like being Alice in Wonderland searching around a world that didn't make sense nor had any directions.

*I don't want to have to figure this out on my own. I want to know how to expedite this process.*

Not only did I feel like I was in a constant state of freefall, but I was filled with angst, waiting for the toxicology report. I would often go down the rabbit hole of "what if" regarding the cause of Kevin's death.

Whether or not it was an overdose loomed over me.

Deputy Brody had called me two days after his initial call to tell me there had been no suspected foul play, and both of the kids' stories checked out. He reminded me that it would take four months for the toxicology report to come back.

It wasn't until all the services were over and the overwhelming grief and silence started to swallow me that the "what if's" arose all around me. Without an actual story of what happened, I started to imagine the possibilities. The number of facts I had of the timeline was very little.

Kevin had been living in northern California and had driven a few hours south on Friday to meet up with his friends, Tim and Adam, who lived in San Francisco.

He had planned to stay for the weekend and go to a couple of music shows.

He arrived late and missed Friday night's show, so all three kids instead went to a party at another location. They all went back to Adam's apartment around 2:00 a.m., smoked pot, and went to bed around 3:00 a.m. Tim and Adam woke up the next morning to find Kevin dead on the futon. They called 911 and performed CPR, but he was already gone. The evidence found in the apartment was a small amount of marijuana and a bottle of whiskey. Tim had told the police that he had a small amount of cocaine on him, but that none of them had used the drug that night. It was later tested by the police and tested positive for morphine.

After I had hung up with Deputy Brody, Tom and I discussed the drugs. I asked if he would please keep quiet about it until we knew more.

"The cause still could have been related to his asthma. I don't want to mention the morphine to our family or anyone until we get the toxicology report back."

"Okay?" I added it to make it sound less demanding.

"Okay. No sense saying anything until we know for sure," Tom said.

In my forty-eight years, I had never personally known anyone who died from an overdose. I kept pleading with God. *Please don't let drugs be the reason for his death.*

When I wasn't at the computer, looking for answers and directions, I was in Kevin's room. I had found Kevin's bedroom to be a place where I could sit with my pain in private—a place to cry, journal, listen to his music, and be surrounded by all that was his. It had been during that first week of preparing for the services when I figured out that I was unable to cry if someone else was crying. If during a conversation, I was crying and the other person started to cry, my tears would stop. I physically was unable to cry *with* anyone except for the dogs. Kevin's room became a place where I could cry for as long as I wanted, which allowed me the luxury of coming completely undone.

His room was located at the furthest point from the back door where everyone entered which allowed me plenty of privacy from anyone stopping by. I wanted to be as close to Kevin as possible, and the most tangible way I could be was to be in his room with all of his things and the faintest, lingering smell of him. His room was small, 11×13 with two windows, one facing north and one facing west. His bed was up against the wall where you could sit and look out the west-facing window and gaze upon a quiet meadow lined with pine, ash and cherry trees. Over the years, in that same meadow, we would see white-tailed deer bounding through to the woods and on a few occasions, black bears sauntering through. On summer evenings, the west-facing window framed the most spectacular sunsets. I imagined that window as a portal connecting me to where his soul resided.

Every morning, I would go in his room, sit on his bed, and look through that window. I'd always announce myself by greeting him.

"Good morning, Kev."

I wanted to always be sure he knew I was there, that I would be spending some time talking to him and wanted him to know I was listening for whispers from him, too.

Although Kevin had the best view in the house, that end got the brunt of the wind that came up the street. Every morning I'd grab a sweater in anticipation when I opened the door, I'd hear the winter winds howling. After making sure both dogs were inside the room with me, I'd shut the door behind us.

I had saved every sympathy card we received and kept them in a large box in the corner of Kevin's room, keeping the ones that had specific stories about Kevin separated so I could reread and savor those scenes I hadn't been present for.

One day, I placed the cards with Kevin stories on the bed and reached down pulling back the blankets exposing the hidden sheets. I crawled into the bed slipping under the covers, fully feeling the weight of the three wool blankets that he liked his bed to have.

He hadn't been home for a year, but I could still smell his scent ever so slightly on his pillow and the blankets. I took a few deep breaths and laid still listening to the wind, wondering if it had lulled Kevin to sleep or kept him awake. I opened my eyes, glanced over at Manny and Tripp, and gave a slight tap of the bed with my hand. It was all the invitation they needed to jump up to join me.

Tripp had nestled himself alongside my waist with his blonde head on my chest while Manny contently laid at my feet. I let the physical weight of the blankets and the dogs against my side and feet do their work to calm my perpetually anxious and grief-laden body. I had brought a few cards into bed with me and reached for one I had received the day before.

It had green lily pads with an ivory-colored lotus flower on the front. I picked at the flower's petals that were made of some sort of stiff parchment paper. Manny gave a deep sigh, taking one last look at me before resting his head on my ankles that were underneath the blankets. I opened the card and read the text.

*Sharing your loss with deepest sympathy.*

My eyes moved to the left-hand side of the card which was full of handwritten print in black pen. I read it out loud to Manny and Tripp while I rhythmically stroked Tripp's ear.

"Dear Mr. and Mrs. Lynch,

... Some of my fondest memories of Kevin were working on the farm with him."

Both dogs momentarily lifted their heads upon hearing Kevin's name. When Kevin was living with us, I used to say, "Kevin's home," and they'd go running to the door.

"His motto when picking berries was 'pick one, eat two,' and it never failed to make us laugh. I think he and I ate more produce than we ever picked. Those were the best days after school when I got to work with him. I have so many fantastic memories of him, and I'll hold them close to my heart ..."

I smiled as I imagined the scene of Kev eating the berries and could taste the salt of my tears when they reached my lips. Learning a new story, even one as small as picking berries on the farm, was like being gifted a new memory, knowing mine were finite.

I rubbed the blonde head closest to me, which was Tripp, per usual. Tripp was almost always the closest whereas Manny was content to be the backup, Tripp's wingman, supporting his efforts. It was as if they had a code between them on how to care for me. Both knew exactly what I needed when I needed it.

After hours of pouring over the cards and crying, my eyes were burning and swollen; I needed to get up. I walked into the bathroom right off Kevin's room, took the gray hand towel off the rack and turned the faucet on, letting the cold water soak the towel. I looked in the mirror while wringing out the towel in the sink barely recognizing my face that was partially distorted from the swelling.

I ran my fingers through my hair in a feeble attempt to comb it.

*Tomorrow needs to be a hair washing day.*

I broke away from my depressing reflection and sat on the side of the tub and pressed the wet towel on my eyes. I could hear the rustling of a dog getting up and their nails on the bedroom floor coming toward me. The clicking stopped for a second, then I heard the familiar swish of a Kleenex being pulled from the box and a few more clicks, and I knew he was next to me. I looked up from the towel to see Manny looking right at me, holding the edge of a fresh tissue with his front teeth.

I looked into his dark brown eyes.

*How do you always know?*

He looked quite pleased with himself knowing he brought me something I needed. I took the tissue, blotted my eyes, and blew my nose, making full use of the gift.

Sitting with my grief in Kevin's room became a sacred daily practice that I came to see as a necessary part of my healing. It became *my plan* to focus on only my grief for a certain amount of time every day. Manny and Tripp would always accompany me, agreeable to patiently lay on the floor or come up onto the bed with me. I never had to hide my feelings from them because there was never any judgment. I confided in them, and in return, they gave me unconditional love.

I never had a particular plan of what I was going to do, but I eventually got into a rhythm of journaling the thoughts, feelings, and experiences I was having and documenting my own stories of Kevin. It was a place to openly grieve since when out in public or at work, I was always trying to keep my emotions in check.

The boxes of pictures we had gone through from the services were still in the living room. I wasn't ready to put them away, so I moved them into Kevin's room, putting them in the corner alongside the box of sympathy cards. Occasionally, I'd reach in and pull out a random picture and would recall the day, then write the memory that went with the photo.

There was a morning I had the urge to really dig through and look at all of them. I walked over to the boxes, picked one out, and put it on his bed. Using the bed as my table, I grabbed a stack of baby pictures sitting at the top of the pile. I picked one of him sleeping peacefully, sucking his thumb in a light blue onesie.

I reached in the box and pulled out another one of him as a toddler with platinum blonde hair. In this one, he was sitting at the kitchen table with a yellow Winnie-the-Pooh cake with a number two candle stuck in yellow frosting. There was another in a red Polo shirt on his first day of preschool at our old house, standing next to sunflowers that were taller than he was.

I thumbed through a small stack of little league baseball pictures and landed on one from when he was ten years old. Kevin and his friends, Cole and Alex, were sitting in our sunroom in their matching gray and blue all-star baseball uniforms. I relived the day in my mind, which ended with us at Hayward's Ice Cream.

I came across the epic picture of him standing on the dock in Provincetown, smiling-with-his-whole-head, holding up the forty-two-inch striped bass. My in-laws had a boat, a fifty-foot Carver, and would take the four of us on weekend boating trips every summer off Cape Cod. When Matthew and Kevin were eleven and nine years old, we had gone by boat from Constitution Marina in Boston Harbor to Provincetown, Massachusetts and spent the weekend. The next morning, Tom had taken Matthew and Kevin out in the dinghy for an early morning fishing excursion while I slept in a bit. When they came back, Tom woke me up and said "Kevin caught a huge striper. You gotta come to see him. He's smiling with his whole head."

I found so many pictures from Lake Winnipesaukee, and I pulled out the one where he was high-fiving Matthew while they water skied side-by-side. Then I found the newer ones as a young adult in Costa Rica where we last saw him alive.

I sat on his bed and lined them up in front of me in order of age like a timeline and touched each one. I remembered taking all of these pictures. Those were times when I could put my camera down and reach out and hug him.

*Just one more. I just want one more hug.*

Thinking of not being able to hug him was like a sucker punch, and I slid off the bed to be closer to Manny and Tripp who had been lying at my feet. Both dogs were unflinching when they heard me wail, letting me sob uncontrollably once again curled up on the floor next to them until I had expelled everything I had. They always stayed with me through these bouts, no matter how long they took. I suddenly felt a surge of conscious gratitude for them.

Day in and day out, for weeks, they continued to hold emotional space for me. Even when I couldn't offer them much, they continued to show up with acceptance and love. Then it happened. A moment after I felt that gratitude for my dogs, an unrelated idea pushed into my awareness.

*You can have a hug anytime you want. You've hugged Kevin a thousand times. You remember all the details. Play it out in your mind.*

My spirits lifted at the idea of us hugging one more time even if it was just in my mind. I wiped my tears and had a second thought.

*Was this really my idea?*

Feeling as if I was getting help from another source, I felt my spirits lift a little more. I sat on the floor thinking about what the hugging scenario would be. I decided to visualize the summer after he graduated from high school. He was heading out to meet his friends at Rocky Pond.

*Yes, he was always extra happy in the summer, especially when going to hang out with friends on a hot summer day by the water.*

I'd imagine he was looking for sunblock, and when I handed him a tube, he'd be overly dramatic, nodding his head with a big smile on his face.

*Alllllrighttttt, Mom! You saved the day!*

It was one thing to plan out an imaginary hug scene in my mind, but it was completely different going through it as a visualization, using all my senses to relive the experience. I stood up and sat back on the bed. Looking out the west window, my portal, I thought *This isn't going to be easy.*

And I was right.

Every morning, for weeks, I'd walk into Kevin's room, sit at my portal, and try to visualize only to find myself lying in his bed crying. I'd be able to get to the point where he was walking toward me and I handed him the sunblock but was having a hard time getting past him saying, "Mom, you saved the day."

I decided to change the scene slightly, and I reimagined the scene in my mind. It was still summer, and he was still going to the pond with friends. I imagined a newer version where we would have a funny exchange, and that made all the difference. I sat at my portal, lit a candle, and took a few deep breaths.

"Good morning, Kev. I'm going to close my eyes and imagine us hugging. I'd love it if you could help me. I'd love for you to do it with me."

I closed my eyes and began.

He was wearing one of his many Grateful Dead t-shirts. This one was more subdued than most of the wild tie-dyed ones. This shirt was navy blue and happened to be my favorite. It had colored teddy bears and turtles dancing by a campfire under the stars with a crescent moon in the distance. He was in tan cargo shorts cinched with a brown braided leather belt. He had low-cut socks, and as always, they were mismatched. He looked directly at me, still smiling, and I couldn't help but feel pride at what a genuine, loving human being he was. I felt his aura expand as he loped toward me, and it reached me well before he did. As his aura washed over me, it felt like I was being embraced by sunshine.

He said, "MOTHERRRRRR ... " letting the "r's" slowly fade as he stretched his long arms wide.

He wrapped his arms around me and lifted me a couple of inches off the ground. His blonde curls were jutting out from under his faded red cap. They lightly brushed my right cheek as the side of his head gently pressed mine. I smelled his damp, freshly shampooed hair and felt his chin on my shoulder. I hugged him back, my fingers pressed into his lean back, feeling the softness of his t-shirt. I said, "Keeevvvvv" in a silly, cartoon-like voice attempting to imitate him from when he was little. We shared a knowing laugh over it as he released me.

I felt every detail. I saw every nuance of his face—the crinkles that appear at the corners of his eyes when he smiled and how his head slightly tilted back when he laughed. I let it all wash over me. When I had thoroughly felt all of it, I was not afraid to end the reunion. I opened my eyes, knowing I could visit with him and hug him anytime I wanted.

Adding laughter to the scene felt right to me. It was nice to even just *imagine* myself laughing again. Before Kevin died, I would laugh easily and often. I'd always felt it was a blessing. I found lots of things funny and have declared many times that laughing is my most favorite thing to do. I would often appreciatively tell Tom, who has always been one of the funniest people I know, that his ability to make me laugh was the number one reason I married him. But back in the physical world, I was starting to think laughter would be what I did during the days *before* Kevin died.

●　●　●

Late January arrived and we woke up to a winter wonderland. Six inches of fresh snow had fallen the night before, and it hadn't stopped yet. I walked to the back door in my bathrobe and opened the door to let the dogs out to potty. Their noses turned upward when they were exposed to the cold air, twitching as if they were trying to sniff a snowflake while they waited for their release out the door.

"Okay," I said, and they dashed out, getting right to business, relieving themselves.

I waited outside for them to finish and watched as they took a couple of bouncing strides away from the fence and flopped down onto their sides, rolling on their backs with their legs kicking in the air, making doggie snow angels. They got up and shook, and I quickly stepped back into the house.

From the threshold, I held the door open and called them in. I looked at their imprints in the snow and couldn't help but think of how excited Kevin was when he was little and it was a snow day.

It reminded me of one winter morning when Kev was about six. It had snowed the night before, and the guy who snowplowed for us had come in the middle of the night. He had pushed the snow from the driveway onto our front lawn, making it three times as deep as it would have been otherwise. When Kevin had woken up, he saw the snow and opted out of breakfast to get outside faster and make snow tunnels. I could see him from the kitchen window busy making his fort.

Thinking back now, it is the only time I can ever remember that he was perfectly content playing alone. He had been out for a couple of hours that morning and came to get me only because he wanted me to take a picture of him in his snow fort.

"This is the best day of my life!" he said after I snapped the picture.

It was a phrase he used often when he was little and was having a great time. I had come across that picture the day I went through the box of photos. In the picture, all you could see was the white of the snow surrounding a six-year-old

Kevin on his hands and knees, peeking out from a tunnel. He was wearing a blue knit Patriots hat, sporting a smile with a missing front tooth.

The dogs were pacing at my feet, which pulled me from the image of Kevin having another *best day of his life* moment. They were letting me know they, too, were excited to get back out to play in the snow.

I walked across the kitchen to the sliding glass door and slid it open. Both dogs waited for the release to go into the fenced-in part of the yard.

"Okay," I said, and they launched into the snow.

I stood watching them through the glass taking turns chasing one another in the snow. I was still in my bathrobe sipping coffee and was content to see them having such a good time from the comfort of my kitchen. I stood there wondering if everything was going to remind me of Kevin. I walked to the sink and dumped the cooled remains of my coffee down the drain and put the cup in the dishwasher.

*I'll let them continue to play while I take a shower.*

The plows would be out soon, which would give them enough time to clear the parking lot at the Beaver Brook trailhead.

*It will be a good time for a walk in the woods.*

When I was finished getting ready, I went to the basement to put on my snow pants and grab my boots and came back upstairs to see both dogs standing at the slider with snowballs stuck to their fur, looking to come in. I opened the door and sat down to put my boots on. I had just finished tying my laces when I looked over and saw Tripp's head resting on his front paws, trying to effectively pant. He was winded from the frenzy he just had outside. His eyes shifted from my boots to my face, anticipating the next words out of my mouth.

"Do you wanna go for a walk?" I asked.

Hearing the word "walk" commanded Tripp's full attention. His ears pricked. His panting ceased as he held his breath, springing up in one smooth motion. He looked directly at me, cocking his head to the side for good measure. His expression said it all.

*Yes, I do! This is the best day of my life!*

I had heard those words so many times, and now I could imagine them in a thought bubble over Tripp's head.

*Tripp reminds me so much of Kevin. It's like he is the canine version of Kevin.*

Then I heard it.

It was laughter. My laughter. For the first time in months.

*Chapter 8*

# The Results Are Posted

*February 2016*

I began swimming competitively when I was eight years old and continued throughout my senior year in high school. Although I was always technically on a team, my experience was that swimming was an individual sport since I focused on competing against myself, always striving to beat my personal best. Before every race, I would know what my best time had been, and I finished every race checking to see if I beat it.

By the time I was eleven, I had been making steady progress improving my stroke, chipping away at my times each meet. At the end of the season, the swim club hosted an awards night at a local Italian restaurant to recognize the accomplishments of the swimmers. Because I had been keeping track of my progress, I felt it was a real possibility I could receive one of the awards, and I wanted to look nice just in case. I chose my favorite green velour top, gray chinos, and brown leather clogs.

My mom and I arrived at the restaurant where the ceremony was being held. As we walked into the private function room in the back, I saw the podium that stood like a beacon in the front of the room. There were rows of tables covered with paper tablecloths where we would eat ravioli smothered in red sauce, rolls, and salad.

After dinner, my coach Ms. Donnavan, walked up to the podium with a folder of papers. I was so nervous when she announced the awards for the eleven- and twelve-year-old age group, hoping I would be getting one.

"This trophy goes to the winner of the Most Improved swimmer ...."

I stood up and walked up to the podium amongst the clapping of my teammates and their parents, feeling a few inches taller. My coach smiled at me. "Congratulations, Susan." She handed me a trophy and certificate then put her hands on my shoulders and gently turned me to face the audience and my mother who had crept up closer to take my picture. When I got back to my seat, I gave the trophy a closer inspection to see my name had been engraved on the bottom.

I handed my mother the certificate. "Mom, can you hold onto this so nothing spills on it?" I wanted to keep the documentation of my accomplishment pristine.

The feeling of external validation was something I craved and that would continue to seep into other areas throughout my life. My grades, scores, times, placements, certificates, degrees, ribbons, titles, and trophies were all clear, tangible measurements of my success and self-worth.

I had forgotten the high I would get with these tangible proofs of my capability—at least until dog training came into the picture. But between my swimming days and the days of dog competition, it was motherhood.

Tom and I met in college when we were both nineteen and fell in love. We were married at twenty-one and had both our children by twenty-three. I was a stay-at-home mom and loved it. Although there wasn't any documentation on how I was doing as a mom, there were many parts of motherhood that I deemed as feedback. When my kids spent time with friends, I heard from the parents, "Your kids are so polite! It's so nice to hear 'please' and 'thank you.'" I would beam with pride every time I heard it.

When Kevin was little and his behavior would take on more of a mischievous turn, he'd offset my frustration with a sincere look of regret on his face, and upon seeing my face he'd look down. He hated when he was called out for disappointing people, even at a young age. It was like kryptonite for him, but he was a natural at figuring out how to get himself back into my good graces.

One time when he was little, he said, "Sorry, Mommy. I will be-a-hay-ve." I was trying to stifle a smile on how cute his rendition of behave was. "You mean 'behave'?" I asked, trying not to laugh. He nodded "yes," his blue eyes clouded with tears. I reached out and pulled him onto my lap and wiped the tear sliding down his cheek. He had me at "be-a-hay-ve."

At some point, I started taking credit for my children's successes or failures because it directly reflected on me. It was like receiving an A+ grade when I heard positive feedback about my kids: when they were complimented for their manners, came home with a good grade on a test, or received a compliment from their teachers or coaches. When they had jobs and their employers were happy with their work, when they were well-liked among their peers, and when they went off to college, I'd give myself an A+.

Conversely, I'd give myself a C when I got a call saying they were talking or being disruptive in class. And with Kevin, I felt helpless when he came back after one year of college feeling like a failure, sank into depression, and was arrested for marijuana possession. I couldn't fix his problems, and I took on the responsibility of being unable to do so. When he seemed to fail, I felt like I failed, too.

With my kids, I was "winning" if they were winning. And the feeling was oddly similar when dogs entered the picture except there were tangible results to hold onto, proving I was good at what I was doing. I had a dog as a kid and always wanted my kids to grow up with a dog. It was an easy sell to Tom as I would be the one taking care of it.

I started taking pet training classes one evening per week when Tom was home from work. At one point my instructor (who competed with her own dogs) pulled me aside and said, "You know Susan, you should really think about doing some competitive obedience training with this dog. You have a knack for it, and I think you guys could do well."

That was all the feedback I needed to sign up.

In dog training, I found a love that touched a fundamental part of me—the little girl who watched *Wild Kingdom* and had a love of nature and animals. Connecting and communicating with my dogs, observing their behavior while being in nature started a lifelong passion.

By the time I brought Manny home, I had been training and competing for over a decade. I had picked him out of a litter of eight mostly based on his ability to make me laugh and the fact he would try to get my attention by making eye contact. If I looked away from him, he'd bark and when I looked back at him, he'd do something silly like shake a toy with his teeth. He'd stop to make sure I was still watching, then toss it and romp over to pick it up and repeat. The day I brought him home I held him in my arms and whispered into his ear, "You, my friend, are going to be an experiment."

Like my previous dogs, I had started training Manny as an eight-week-old puppy. Manny and I laid the foundation for both obedience and retriever training or "field" as we called it. I'd start every January by setting goals of specific titles I wanted to accomplish for the year. I'd go online and search and map out which tests and shows I'd want to travel to and write them onto my calendar. We trained in the field year-round even when there was snow on the ground.

After my kids graduated from high school, dog training became a wonderful cushion for the empty nest blues I was feeling. Manny and I had been training with Rick, a professional field trainer, every week, preparing for hunt tests. Under his tutelage, we reached the level of Master Hunter by the time Manny was four years old.

Rick had been encouraging me to run Manny in a competitive retriever test called Qualifying. A Qualifying stake was difficult like a Master Hunter test, but you competed against other dog/handler teams for placements as opposed to a hunt test where you competed against a written standard where you either passed or failed.

The following spring, Manny and I were a solid team in advanced training concepts. At the end of a spring training session with Rick, I was loading Manny into my truck when he walked over to me.

"You and Manny are ready to run a Qualifying," he said matter-of-factly.

His words washed over me, giving me that wonderful feeling of acknowledgment. I knew him well enough to know he wouldn't have made the statement unless he meant it.

When I arrived home, I went right to my computer and found a Qualifying stake that was to be held on a Friday with a Master Hunt test on Saturday and Sunday near Lake Champlain in bucolic Vermont. I figured since the drive was more than three hours from my house, I'd enter both the Qualifying stake and Master Hunter test and make it a three-day weekend.

I had been spending hunt test weekends with my "dog friends" for several years as Manny went up the ranks from Junior to Senior then Master. We had finished our Master title, but it would be fun to see them and tailgate at the end of the day.

We arrived on a Thursday evening and got situated in a cheap motel that took dogs. My nervousness about the Qualifying started as soon as I arrived. The morning of the test I woke before my alarm went off. I packed up Manny, left the motel at 7:00 a.m., and stopped at the village store on the way to the test headquarters to get a cup of Vermont's famous Green Mountain coffee and a sandwich for later.

I left the store, sipping my coffee, and drove to the Dead Creek Wildlife Management area, taking in the classic New England countryside of red barns, metal silos, and huge green pastures dotted with black and brown dairy cows. The headquarters was where the handlers met at the beginning of test day to get directions to the field where the first series was going to be held. I arrived at the test headquarters, parked in the shade, and opened the tailgate and cap window to give Manny some air. When I walked over to the chief marshal to get the handout with the address, I heard a noise from behind. I turned around to see that a van had just hit the back corner of my truck.

"Oh my God! I'm so sorry!" the driver shouted out her van window, quickly pulling forward.

*Oh shit! Manny!*

I ran to my truck to check on him and found him standing in his crate. I opened his crate door and carefully picked him up and placed him on the ground. As soon as I let go of him, he was wagging his tail and whining, wanting to say hello to the people who had run over to make sure we were okay.

After a few minutes of checking him over, we determined he was absolutely fine. I put him back in his crate and gingerly closed the tailgate to make sure it could shut. The driver of the van was standing next to me visibly shaken.

"I am so sorry ... The sun was in my eyes ... I didn't see your truck ... Are you sure he's okay?"

"Yes, he's fine, and the door even shuts," I said. "Let's exchange contact information, and we can deal with it after the test, okay?"

"Yes. Okay. Um, I'm so very sorry," she said sincerely.

"It was an accident. I am going to think of it as ... a good luck kiss," I said and smiled at her, then climbed into my truck and turned the key.

I arrived at the test grounds and scanned the handlers who had gathered to hear the few bits of details on the mechanics for the day. It was an owner-handler Qualifying, meaning professional handlers could only run their own dogs.

Most of the amateur handlers entered were "field trialers," meaning they didn't typically run in the non-competitive hunt tests. Although we had been running in hunt tests for a few years, this was only the second Qualifying I'd ever seen.

I had watched the teams run before me and noted the excitement and precision of the dogs working. We were the nineteenth dog to run, and as we walked up to the line,

I briefly heard whispers from the spectators, but I shut them out as I approached the starting line.

I had bathed Manny that week, so he looked extra fluffy against the other retrievers that were entered. Manny was excited and somewhat fed my nervousness by walking slightly ahead of me. I gave him a stern "sit" as he reached the starting line which allowed me to close the gap by taking one more step to stand alongside him. As soon as I was next to him, we both switched gears and settled into our jobs, shaking off any nervousness.

I had previously seen the test dog run (a dog not entered that runs the series) which highlighted details not visible from the line; the dips in the terrain, where bird scent would gather, and other pitfalls of the test. I did a quick scan of the field to look for movement of the grass and tree leaves to note the wind direction. Looking down at the top of Manny's head, I could see his eyebrows moving, looking back and forth at the three separate bird stations out in the field.

His shifting eyes were an indication that he was trying to decide on which bird he would pick up first. To remind him this was a team effort and help him to settle, I said, "Sit. Mark." ("Mark" is a term used to indicate to the dog that something is about to be thrown to retrieve). When he looked out at the long bird station, I slowly and quietly said, "Yeeeessss. Right there," and with that, he leaned slightly forward with his eyes locked on it. I had successfully gotten my message across.

"Yesssss," I repeated, making sure he had a good look at the long mark. "Mark." Then silently, I gave a low wave behind my back to signal the judges we were ready.

He retrieved all three marks perfectly and we walked off the line with more whispers from the spectators. He had a small hiccup in the second series but redeemed himself in the third series. I had watched most of the teams run and felt Manny and I had a real chance to be in the ribbons.

When the fourth and final series was over, it was dusk. The handlers gathered to wait while the judges deliberated, privately scribbling on the scoresheets resting on their clipboards. When the judges were finished, they handed the placements over to the chief marshal, waving a clipboard in the air. "Gather up everyone. The results are posted!"

All the handlers quieted.

The chief marshal addressed the small crowd. "On behalf of the Lake Champlain Retriever Club, I'd like to thank our judges for their time and expertise with our test today."

We all clapped. Those of us who were still in contention knew any placement was a huge accomplishment to be celebrated. The expression "second place sucks" does not apply here.

I knew they would call out dog and handler team numbers and was so nervous I suddenly forgot what my number was. I picked up my entry catalog and scanned the twenty other entries.

*Oh, right. Number 19, my birthday number.*

"In fourth place is dog and handler number 19," and the gallery started clapping again. I stood up and thought my shaking knees would give out as I walked up to receive the white rosette. When the rest of the placements had been awarded, I went back to my truck and let Manny out for a hug.

Because it was dark, a celebratory walk was out of the question, so I loaded him back into his crate and headed back to the motel. I spread out a sheet I packed to keep dog hair off the bed and sat on the side, patting the space beside me. He jumped up and laid on his back for some well-deserved belly rubs as I drank my celebratory beer. I took a long shower then shared my dinner of chicken fingers and French fries with him.

I crawled into bed, my body a little sunburned and exhausted from a day full of adrenaline. I rolled over and looked into his dark brown eyes and was overcome once again with emotion.

"You did a great job today, Manny," and I kissed his muzzle. I settled into my pillow and felt his head rest on my shoulder as if to say, "You did too, Mom," and the both of us drifted off to sleep.

That placement, along with the major win toward his breed championship he had received two months prior, would meet the requirements for Manny to be entered into the Golden Retriever Club of America's (GRCA) prestigious Dual Dog Hall of Fame. He would also be awarded the GRCA's Bill Lester trophy that year for his accomplishments in both field and conformation. He would then hold the honor as the fifth dog in the 30+ years of GRCA history to be a Champion, a Master Hunter, and have a field trial placement.

●　●　●

As the four-month mark loomed for the toxicology report, I started taking the dogs out for a walk in the morning. The mailman was coming at lunchtime, and I wanted to make sure I was home when he arrived. I could see the mailbox from my kitchen window, but even with the windows closed, I could hear the droning sound of the truck's motor slowing down, then picking up after the mail was deposited.

When the truck was out of sight, I'd take the one-hundred-foot walk to the black box at the end of my driveway. Each time I stood in front of it, I'd hold my breath. My fate was already determined; I just didn't know what it was. I had a constant inner conflict.

In one ear, I'd hear *It doesn't change anything, it doesn't bring him back*, and in the other ear, I'd hear *how he died will determine how he is remembered by people and how they would view me as a mother.*

On a snowy day in February, I heard that now-familiar sound of the mailman driving past my house. I put my boots on and made the walk down my driveway. I paused and took a deep breath, sucking in the cold air and slowly exhaling, hoping it would somehow push the fear out of me.

It did not.

I grabbed the tab on the top of the door and pulled it down. I could see right on the top of the pile was a plain white envelope with a return address from California.

It was here.

*The results are posted*, echoed somewhere in the back of my mind.

If it was an asthma attack, I would know it couldn't have been prevented. I had taken him to the ER several times over the years during severe attacks, so I knew how bad his breathing could get. I knew it could lead to death. If the cause was asthma there would have been nothing I or anyone else could have said or done to prevent it from coming on. If drugs were involved, I could envision myself slipping into magical thinking filled with thoughts starting with "what-ifs" and "I-should-haves." My mind would be tricked into thinking I had the power all along to change the outcome.

I pulled the contents out and quickly made my way back to the house. My coat fell into a heap on the floor as I pulled it off, and I left my boots askew on the rug as I went straight to the bedroom with the envelope, shutting myself in alone.

Manny and Tripp laid down on the other side of the door; I heard their elbows hit the wood floor. I was home alone, but I locked my door anyway. I sat on my bed and carefully opened the envelope.

Sheriff's Office

M E M O R A N D U M

Autopsy performed on the body of Kevin Lynch at the coroner's bureau ...

AUTOPSY FINDINGS

1. BLOOD ETHYL ALCOHOL
2. BLOOD MORPHINE
3. BLOOD CODEINE
4. BLOOD 6-MAM PRESENT

CAUSE OF DEATH: MULTIPLE DRUG INTOXICATION

The only part of my body that could move was my eyes. I read and reread the autopsy findings.

I knew he had been drinking and stopped looking at number one.

*The blood had tested positive for morphine.*

*Tim said none of them did any that night. What is 6-MAM?*

*How can codeine be listed and wasn't found by the police?*

*How could morphine and codeine be in his system, and no one saw him take anything? Did Kevin even know what he was taking?*

I didn't understand what I was looking at. I didn't know how drugs metabolize in the body. How would I know? I was just a mother looking for answers as to what happened to her son.

I got up, unlocked the door, and went to my computer. I brought up Google and typed in 'What is 6-MAM?' and hit return.

*When someone uses heroin, the drug is converted into the active metabolite 6-MAM, which can be found for several hours after heroin use. 6-MAM is a unique metabolite of heroin.*

I stared at my computer screen, looking at the word "heroin" for what seemed like hours.

*How could I not know he was using these kinds of drugs?*

*How am I going to tell my parents? My family? My friends? What are they going to think of him? What will they think of me? What did I do wrong?*

I felt sick to my stomach and ran to the bathroom to vomit.

Sitting on the bathroom floor, my head was spinning. I couldn't organize my thoughts. I laid down on the cold tile as feelings of panic and shame gripped me tight. I laid there until the tile was no longer cold and my nausea started to subside. I sat up and tried to collect my thoughts.

*Where do I even start to unravel all of this? I don't have any information except this piece of paper.*

Anger crept its way in. The lack of information angered me as much as the information I did have. I slid the paper across the floor; I didn't want it near me.

Blame wasn't my objective; I only wanted an explanation of what happened. Tim and Adam could never have imagined the consequences of partying that night and of the horror that would greet them when they woke up. Certainly, the two of them and their parents were experiencing their own levels of grief and trauma around what happened that night. I had compassion for all of us, but I was his mother, and no one could tell me what happened.

I wanted more of an explanation.

I picked up the piece of paper, knowing I needed the phone number at the top. Still feeling a bit queasy, I walked to the bedroom, locked the door, and picked up my cell phone that was on the bed.

*I will request a copy of the autopsy report.*

Sitting down on the bed, I started tapping into my phone the number to the coroner's office and put a hand on my stomach while it rang.

"Hello. My name is Susan Lynch. I'd like the full autopsy report of my son Kevin Lynch."

"Date of death please?" a woman asked.

"October 3, 2015."

"Hold on, please." She put me on a brief hold. "We charge five dollars to mail the report."

"Okay. I can give you my credit card number."

"We only take cash," she said flatly, seemingly unfeeling.

"I am on the east coast. Would it be possible for you to please send it, and I will mail you the cash? This is my son's autopsy," I reminded in case she didn't pick up on it at the beginning of the call.

"No, I'm sorry. We will send it out when we receive the cash," she said as if this was a question she heard often from next of kin.

She was no better than Karen from the bank.

*Why doesn't anyone care about my son's death?*

She gave me the address, and I hung up.

I stuffed a five-dollar bill into an envelope along with my name and address and promptly drove the envelope to the post office.

Two weeks later, a large manilla envelope contained sixteen pages of details of the autopsy with the receipt for the $5.00 payment stapled to the front. I spent days pouring over every page. I don't know what I was looking for. I just knew a list of drugs wasn't enough for me.

I looked up the technical medical terms and descriptions, looking for any details to help me piece together what happened. One morning I took my coffee in the room opposite Tom. I didn't want him to see me still obsessing over the report. He had had enough when he saw the shortlist.

I had just settled into the overstuffed chair with my coffee in one hand and the report in the other when Tripp walked by and bumped my hand holding the coffee mug splashing the contents on the front page of the report. I jumped up and ran the wet packet to the sink, shaking off the excess and blotting with a dish towel to no avail. The coffee had stained and wrinkled the first few pages. I put the wet document on the kitchen table to dry. The fact that the toxicology report was on the top and that it was a mess was not lost on me.

# Chapter 9

# Exercise Finished

*March 2016–April 2016*

The time spent waiting for the toxicology results had me in a state of limbo, but once I had learned the results, it had me questioning my self-worth, among other things. My feelings surrounding the results were so intense they needed to be dealt with slowly and privately. Not telling anyone ended up being my first real decision regarding my future. The second was to start assessing what of my old life was still working and what was not. The biggest thing was determining if dog training and competing were going to remain a priority for me.

Tripp had been in and out of obedience training for the past four years, but because we had been so focused on getting his Master Hunter title, we had not entered a formal obedience show. I knew we would need a few classes to "dust us off" (an expression some competitive dog trainers use when bringing a dog out of retirement), but it was also to see if this part of my identity would survive as part of my new normal.

The week leading up to the show, my competitive nature took over, and I started to cram more training in by going to extra classes and even adding two private lessons. In addition to the time spent getting instruction, there was also time spent practicing out of class. Seven days leading up to the show, my focus was strictly on practicing footwork and precision, which left no time for sitting with my pain.

The morning of the show, we left at 5:00 a.m. It was common for me to leave in the zero-dark-thirty hour as traveling long distances was a normal part of this canine world I was in. Since I stress more when I'm rushed, I always liked to give myself plenty of time to get to any dog event. The drive to Maine was going to take three hours, not including any bathroom breaks; and they were starting at 10:00 a.m., so we needed to leave early.

I put my coffee cup in the sink and took a final scan of the kitchen to make sure I hadn't left a bag behind. I had already made several trips down the basement stairs to the garage, loading the car with Tripp's travel crate, my obedience bag, and extra water. I just needed to grab the dog cookies and my bagged lunch from the fridge.

"Okay, Tripp. Let's go," I said.

On "let's go," Manny slipped through the door and raced down the basement stairs ahead of us.

"Sorry, Manny. Not today," I said standing at the top of the stairs. "We will be home later, buddy."

He didn't look at all like he believed me, standing at the bottom of the stairs, determined to wait for me to come down to open the garage door.

"I'm so sorry, Manny," I said more softly and walked down the stairs to get him. He clearly wasn't coming back up on his own.

I offered him a cookie as an apology. Closing the door, my last glance was of him standing over an uneaten cookie on the floor. I'd never seen him refuse a cookie; he was clearly disappointed. Tripp, on the other hand, practically dove into his crate in the truck.

Looking over my shoulder, backing out of the garage, I could see Tripp standing, wagging his tail in approval. But as I navigated the dark backroads to the highway, all I could see was Manny's face. A heaviness crept over me like someone had just put a lead blanket over my shoulders.

*What's happening?*

As soon as I thought about it, I knew the answer.

I hadn't sat with my grief all week. It had just found me and was settling in for the long ride. Manny's face—that look of confusion, sadness, depression, and disbelief about being left behind—mirrored perfectly how I felt about Kevin leaving me. The thought of not bringing Manny and making him feel how I was always feeling these days, especially after all he had done for me, was all it took to open a floodgate of tears. Grief hit me with unexpected ferocity.

I could have turned around to go home, which would have been the logical thing to do, but nothing about my life was logical. So, I kept driving and cried all the way to the show because, if anything, I knew how to drive and cry.

By the time I reached the show site, I was physically and emotionally exhausted. I parked far enough away from the main entrance to try and compose myself. Squeezing my eyes shut didn't stop that familiar burning feeling that lived in there, and one glance at myself in the rearview mirror proved it.

*I look as bad as I feel.*

I shifted my swollen eyes away from the mirror and to Tripp who was standing in his crate excited about the prospect of being at a show. He had been on enough road trips to know we were at a dog show plus he had seen his blue and white fleece tug toy peeking out of my obedience bag in the back seat. Again, I contemplated going home, but when I looked over my shoulder to back up my truck, I saw Tripp's look of hopeful anticipation and opted to stay. The thought of disappointing another of my dogs was too much.

The show site was in a school gymnasium, and although I had shown there in the past, it was Tripp's first time. He looked as if he was walking on his tiptoes with excitement, which made me feel more than a little guilty that I hadn't been training and showing which both my dogs had considered fun.

We had yet to even get into the building, and I was already having a much harder time than I anticipated. But I couldn't turn around now—not with knowing how happy Tripp was to be here. I had to at least try.

I walked in with my head down, averting my eyes for fear of making eye contact with anyone. I was extra fragile and knew it wasn't the time to have a public exchange with someone who hadn't heard or who wanted to offer condolences. I knew it wouldn't take much for me to come undone again, and on that day, I was hoping to at least *try* to focus on Tripp and the trial.

As an attempt to get in the right headspace, I had started to warm up by doing a little heeling with Tripp. There was a small, matted area to practice, but every time I got going, I had to stop. I kept making mistakes. I hadn't given him the right cue before starting, or I started with the wrong foot, or my about-turn was too abrupt. My focus was on my inner critic who kept pointing out that not only was I unable to get my shit together, it was also futile to keep trying. I again contemplated walking out the door to leave, but instead, I sat down and waited for our class to start.

At 10:00 a.m., the judge called for handlers to watch the "run through," which is done by a person not entered in the show who walks the heeling pattern without a dog to show the handlers what it will look like. As I watched, I tried to imagine Tripp and myself doing the heeling pattern together.

There were a few dog and handler teams ahead of us, so I sat back down to conserve my energy. I was so tired. I made a mental note of the handler with the blonde hair and her black and tan Doberman Pinscher who were in front of us. After about forty minutes, I saw them heading toward the ring. I stood and started rummaging through my training bag, looking for Tripp's leash.

*Where is it? I just had it.*

My chair, Tripp's crate, and my bag were all within four feet of each other.

*How could I have lost his leash?*

I wanted to scream, and just then, I saw the black braided leash on the floor in front of my chair. It must have fallen off my lap when I stood to look in my bag.

*Oh my God, Susan. Get it together.*

I clipped the leash to his buckle collar and went ring-side. I had no plan and no warmup, and the lingering effects of the lead blanket were still weighing on me. Tripp was giving me a look of "let's do this," which raised my spirits only slightly. I mustered a feeble smile and kissed the top of his head.

"I love you, Tripp," I said.

"Dog and handler number 17," the steward said and with that, we stepped in the ring.

Standing in the ring with Tripp by my left side, we listened as the judge gave his brief welcome. I reached down and rubbed his ear, which always made him look up at me so I could scratch under his chin. That gave me the reset I needed, allowing my mind to drop the past five hours to concentrate on the next five minutes. And for the next five minutes, it was as if Tripp and I were the only two beings in the room.

"Forward," the judge said, then watched, jotted something down, and paused.

"Halt."

Pause.

"Forward. Left turn."

Pause.

"Halt," said the judge again.

The last exercise was the recall. The recall is when the handler leaves their dog in a sit position, tells them to stay, and walks to the other end of the ring approximately fifty feet away, then turns to face their dog. The judge proceeds to guide the handler through the last phases of the exercise.

"Sit your dog," the judge said.

"Sit," I said to Tripp.

"Leave your dog," the judge instructed.

I gave Tripp a hand signal to stay and made every effort to briskly walk to the other side of the ring. When I turned to face him, my eyes caught his. He sat leaning forward with his eyes riveted on me, waiting for me to call him. Emotion instantly welled in my throat seeing the love and effort in his eager expression.

"Call your dog," said the judge, which meant he wanted me to call Tripp and expected Tripp would promptly come and sit facing me.

"Tripp, front," I croaked.

Tripp ran to me, closing the fifty-foot gap between us in what seemed like three strides, landing his front perfectly.

I waited for the judge to give me the last signal.

"Finish your dog," the judge said, which meant Tripp would have to move his body promptly and sit on my left side until the judge said "exercise finished."

I lifted my left hand giving a quick hand signal, and Tripp promptly moved his backend and scooted it around to sit perfectly straight alongside me.

"Exercise finished," said the judge.

I had been completely unaware of anyone or anything other than Tripp and the judge's voice giving me the instructions I so desperately wanted in my life. But something about hearing the words "exercise finished" felt like I had just received a message from the Universe. Looking back, I would now call it clairsentience; my inner guidance was aligning with what I wanted. I had just been given permission to stop showing.

We waited as the judge added up the scores, then all the qualifiers were called back into the ring with their dogs. He then took a few moments to address the spectators to explain the qualifying score range.

"This is an AKC Novice class. A perfect score is a 200, and a score of 170 and above is a qualifying score. You need to have three qualifying scores to be awarded the AKC Companion Dog title," the judge explained.

The judge then turned to the qualifiers and called the dog and handler team that he awarded fourth place, then third place, then second place. I knew Tripp had done a really good job, so my adrenaline was starting to flow in anticipation of hearing who won the class.

"Our first-place dog and handler team is also the Highest Scoring Dog in Trial (HIT) today and goes to dog and handler number 17 with a score of 198.5."

Upon hearing my number, I stepped forward and was mildly aware of some clapping as the steward approached me with our ribbons.

Among the ribbons was a prize for Tripp, a stuffed yellow star toy that the steward handed me. Tripp immediately clamped his teeth around it and backed up trying to initiate a game of tug, which I didn't have the energy for so I let it go. Tripp shook it back and forth in his teeth. I was overwhelmed with the range of emotions that had started to bubble up.

That smiling star had thrust me back to Kevin's funeral standing in the front row of the church on that warm October day, listening to Matthew's eulogy "... Shall we pet and hug a dog, my brother? ... Shall we have the courage to embrace and accept what was, what is, and the unexpected of what will be, my brother? ... May you find in the stars a paradise at least as good as the one that you perceived on this earth."

I stood there looking at that yellow star remembering Kevin as among the stars.

On the drive home, I took a contemplative look at the events of the past week. I was certainly happy we won, but had it been worth the emotional roller coaster? My emotions were already chaotic, so why had I added more to my plate? I loved training and showing, but the truth was I wasn't ready to be back. That adrenaline-rushing edge to performing was no longer in reach or even in my purview. Whatever need I previously had to compete was now gone. There was so much more for me to process privately, and I would give myself as much time as I needed to do so. I could go back to competing if I ever changed my mind, but on that drive home, my inner knowing told me it was my last show indefinitely.

As a part of making the commitment to myself and my emotional health, I decided I needed a tangible and symbolic release of this part of my life. The only tangible things I had were more than twenty years' worth of ribbons. So, once I was home, I went to the guest room where my ribbons were hung. A small smile spread across my face looking at their array of colors and feeling the smooth silk tails.

I took them down and spread the pile out on the living room floor, allowing myself to reminisce over the special moments with all four of my dogs, Bailey, Luxa, Manny, and Tripp, and the difference each one had made in my life. The ribbons were a representation of time I spent learning about each one as an individual, but I no longer needed to keep them as proof of the love and connection between us.

During my trip down memory lane, I decided to keep two ribbons, the small green qualifying one from Tripp's High in Trial win and the fourth-place rosette awarded to Manny from the Qualifying field trial.

When I was finished going through the years of memories, I sealed all but the two I was saving in a box. I had learned that the director of a local 4-H club was looking for ribbons to refurbish for the kids in their program. On a warm day in June, Tom and I strapped the box to the back of his motorcycle and took a ceremonious ride to meet with the 4-H director.

"I hope the kids will get as much pleasure receiving these as I did earning them," I said as I handed her the box.

"Thank you so very much. They will be thrilled," she said appreciatively.

I walked back to the bike empty-handed. Tom was waiting for me, leaning up against the seat.

"I just gave her twenty years of memories," I said wistfully, feeling a pang of regret.

"No, you didn't. You still have them," he said.

And he was right.

Those ribbons didn't prove what I had or hadn't done. I didn't need them to show I was successful or good at showing and training. Ultimately, it didn't even matter if I was good at either. My connection with Manny and Tripp and the dogs before them was the most important part. The proof was in our bond.

*Chapter 10*

# Bad Ways to Die

*April 2016–August 2016*

With dog training completely out of the picture, I became focused on my healing and because I had decided to keep the cause of death a secret from everyone—family and friends included—it was extra complicated. I needed time to process my feelings around the cause before I shared it with anyone else. Plus, we still didn't have any information as to how it happened. I had been struggling with both and told Tom I still wasn't ready to tell anyone.

"I'm not ready to share this," I said.

"Okay. We just won't offer any information," he had replied.

I didn't know it at the time, but that decision gave my shame exactly what it needed to thrive—secrecy. I hadn't gone to a therapist because that would require one who had been through child loss. How would I even search for that requirement? I was, however, ready to try a grief support group, but finding the right one was a process.

I arrived at the meeting location feeling about as fragile as a person could get. I slowly walked into the building following the signs that read "Grief Support Group" with arrows that pointed me to a room with about thirty people sitting around a large table talking amongst themselves. The lights in the room seemed extra bright, prompting me to quickly find a seat to stop the feeling of being on a stage. The leader introduced herself and instructed us all to say a little bit about why we had come. I was already feeling like this may not be the right place for me since most people were talking to the person next to them like it was a business meeting. When it was my turn, I felt everyone's eyes on me under the bright lighting of the room. All I could get out was "My son died" and I hid my face in my hands. The woman next to me took the cue that my response had finished and offered up her name and that her grandparent had recently passed away.

The people who were in this group were grieving loved ones who were of the appropriate age to die. I sat through the whole meeting, listening with my head down and with a wad of paper towels covering my face, listening for anything to resonate with me, but it didn't. This group was not for me, and I couldn't wait to leave.

At the end of the meeting, I slipped my arm in the sleeve of my jacket when I felt a hand on my free arm. The group's leader was looking at me with a sympathetic face knowing I was trying to make a quick exit.

"This group isn't for you," she said. "You need a grief group specifically for parents who have lost a child. There is one that meets next week," and she handed me a single piece of paper with the meeting details. "Your grief is very specific, and this is a general grief group," she said. I nodded my head, not trusting I could comment much more than a "thank you" without falling apart. I folded the paper and put it in my coat pocket. I managed a "thank you" and left.

The support group for parents who had lost a child met at a church. I could only assume it was the only available space to meet because it was clearly stated on the flyer they didn't have any religious affiliation.

On the night of the meeting, I arrived ten minutes early and waited in my car, watching people walk in towards the big stone church and follow a narrow walkway to the side door. Most people walked in alone, but I did see one couple walking in together.

*All these people have a child that died.*

"Kev, should I go in?"

I felt like he would want me to at least try.

"Come with me, okay?"

I mustered up some courage, pulled the car door handle, stepped out, and started for the side door. A woman held the door, and we both gave each other a sad smile. I tentatively followed behind her down the hallway and into the meeting room.

The lighting was dim, which was a welcome contrast to the bright, fluorescent lighting of the other group. A small welcome table with coffee and cookies was just past the threshold. An older woman who was pouring herself a cup of coffee looked up at me and said hello.

"Hi," I said.

She introduced herself and her child by gesturing to the pin she was wearing of a smiling teen. When she looked back at me smiling, I could tell her son had inherited her smile.

"Did you have a son or daughter pass?" she said sounding like this would be a completely normal question to ask someone.

"A son," I said quietly.

"I'm so sorry. Recent?"

"Yes, a few months ago," I said.

"Oh," her tone got softer. "I don't know what I would do without this group. Everyone here is so supportive ... and gets it."

I nodded like I knew what she was talking about.

She put her hand on my shoulder. "I'm sorry you are here, but I'm glad you found us."

I could hear people talking behind me, and she looked just past me and waved to someone who had just arrived. "See you in a few minutes in the circle. Oh. And don't forget to sign in," she said gently, squeezing my arm in solidarity and walked past me to greet her friend with a hug. I glanced around the room and didn't know or recognize one person.

*We're all here because we have this one horrible thing in common. I bet there isn't one of us with the same hobby.*

I walked toward the six-foot banquet table covered with a white tablecloth with a clipboard laying on top. The paper on the clipboard was divided into two parts: on the left side was a sign-in sheet, and on the right side was a sign-out sheet for those wanting to borrow a book.

I signed my name on the sign-in side and picked up one of the books: *The Unspeakable Loss: How Do You Live After a Child Dies?*. I put the book down quickly as if it had just burned my hand and cautiously glanced at the rest of the book titles, all of which had words that shouldn't be used in the same sentence.

I looked away from the table not wanting to let myself get pushed too far. My emotions were already teetering between somewhat composed and complete meltdown. I noticed several parents hovering over another folding table and walked over to see what they were looking at.

On the table were about fifty or more photo buttons much like the ones from the '70s that had yellow smiley faces, but instead, these had a real person's face smiling on them.

I had a similar button given to me by Kevin's preschool when he was five years old. The school's photographer had instructed each child to fold their arms in the same way and lean into the crook of a tree on the school's playground. Kevin had on a light blue Polo shirt that made his blue eyes seem bluer and had a smile so big it reached his eyes.

*He always smiled with his whole head.*

The woman standing beside me gave one of the buttons a sad smile when she saw her child's face among the others. She picked it up and pinned it to her shirt, adjusting it to make sure it was straight. I turned away from all the beautiful children's faces, unable to stomach what we all faced, and saw a couple of parents exchanging hugs near metal folding chairs arranged in a circle.

*I don't want one of those buttons.*

A single white candle rested on a small wooden table in the middle of the circle of chairs, and everyone was invited to be seated. The lead blanket of grief crept over me, resting its full weight on top of my shoulders. I was starting to be familiar with being blindsided by it, but I was never ready for its intensity. It was like I had no control over my life.

I had chosen to be at this meeting, but now I wanted to leave. Standing frozen on the outside of the circle, I started to sob, hiding my face in my hands like a child who thinks no one can see her. When a hand rested on my shoulder to gently lead me to a chair, I felt somewhat relieved that I was being shown what to do versus being asked "Are you okay?"

My behavior here was nothing out of the ordinary. Sitting in this circle of chairs felt comforting compared to the other grief group that had us around a boardroom style table under bright lights.

Like the other grief group, we began by introducing ourselves, saying our child's name, their age, when they died, and how they died. The children ranged in ages from infants to middle-aged adults, but they were all someone's child. I sat crying for all of us—me, Kevin, and all the parents sitting in this circle of grief.

I was the last to go, thankfully, but when I came to share, I said only my name, Kevin's, and when he died, not how. They paused as though I weren't finished, but I didn't relent. I was not sharing how he died.

Each meeting, after the introductions, were discussions around a specific topic. For example, we had open discussions about coping with milestones like birthdays and the anniversaries of their deaths or other typically memorable occasions that could be triggering such as graduation, prom, and vacations, to name a few. Sometimes it was just the change of seasons that would be crippling, and we talked about that, too.

At one meeting I brought up how I had been blindsided on the first hot day after Kevin had died. Before he had died, hot summer days would have Kevin happily rummaging through closets, looking for a beach towel and last year's bathing suit. He'd flash me a megawatt smile with a "See ya later, Mom!" and dash out the door to meet friends at Rocky Pond. Something as benign as a shift in the weather had elicited a memory that left me in a puddle of tears on the kitchen floor.

They were a roomful of strangers, but I felt a connection to them much like I would imagine war veterans feel towards each other. We had all been through the trauma of outliving our children. It was the only place I felt like I was seen and heard by people who understood the depth of my grief.

I came to this group for several months and learned a lot. I learned about magical thinking and how to know when you were doing it. Magical thinking happens when a person believes they are somehow responsible for the death because they didn't do enough or know what the right thing was that could have prevented it. Sentences starting with "I should have …," "If only …," and "If I had just …" were ones to watch out for.

If only I had forbidden him to get that motorcycle.

If only I had taken her for a second opinion.

I should have pushed harder to get him into therapy.

If I had just taken her keys, she wouldn't have been in the accident.

I should have known how to help him.

These were good catchphrases to be aware of that pointed out the magical thinking that with more effort or if we had done something differently, we could have changed the outcome. My own magical thinking often appeared as *"At what point did I do the wrong thing? At what point did I stop being a good Mom?"*

Responding to someone's loss by starting the sentence with "At least" instantly minimizes the loss and comes across like the family member should be looking on the bright side.

At least you have another child.

At least you can have more children.

At least you have grandchildren.

At least your son was older when he died.

It was one thing to find your own way to the bright spots, but it was entirely different when someone tried to force it on you with platitudes.

I also learned practical things like to always have an exit plan. If you were going to an event, don't carpool, either drive yourself or take a rideshare service. That way if it gets too much you can just slip out to leave. I appreciated and welcomed any practical advice or tools, feeling it was the closest I'd ever come to having the directions I had been seeking. I continuously asked the more seasoned members specific questions I wanted answers for. The one ever pressing on my mind since Kevin had died was *Is my life just going to be something to endure?*

So, I posed that question to the group and the answer I got surprised me. This parent's child had died decades ago, and she continued to come to the meetings to offer support to other parents who were new to child loss. When her grief was fresh, she had people to help her and now she was paying it forward. She felt that even if she gave hope to only one person it would be worth her time. "Helping other parents is part of my healing process," she said.

*She is still healing?*

I wasn't sure if I should be grateful she had used the word *healing*, letting me know healing was still possible, or be angry that she didn't use the word *healed*, letting me know there was no completing it. I was still in the processing phase, but I tucked away her words of wisdom for my future self.

The biggest benefit of those meetings was the feeling of my grief being seen by people who understood. I saw my pain in their faces and it was something I needed yet couldn't get from a person who hadn't been through it.

But on some level, I felt there was some kind of grief hierarchy. I found myself getting caught up categorizing who had the right to the most sympathy. Whose circumstances were the worst in the sea of tragedies among us?

As sad as my circumstances were, there were parents who lost more than one child, who lost all their children, or whose children's bodies were never found. I believed these parents had an additional element of pain based on their circumstances, which tugged hard at my heart. The circumstances surrounding the cause of death factored in, too—the ones who died from no fault of their own from accidents, illness, or murder versus those who died by suicide and those who were involved in lifestyles that involved high-risk behaviors like drug use. It seemed the former were more noble ways to pass on while the latter were somehow shameful, sinful, or scandalous. Whether anyone else in the group actually thought this or felt it, I didn't really know, but it was something I felt. For that reason, I never told the group how Kevin died.

Years later, after learning more about child loss, I came to understand how complicated this kind of grief was—that no matter what the cause or circumstances surrounding a child's death, each one of us had a tangled knot of emotions to work through within our own story. No two knots were the same. Even the parents of the same child had different feelings surrounding it, which I knew to be true even inside my own marriage.

Tom didn't feel the pull to be around other parents who had experienced child loss whereas I took comfort in being around them. Other than Tom and my dogs, this group of people were the only ones I felt had an understanding of the magnitude of my pain. Another big difference between Tom and me was that he didn't often talk about how he felt. I, on the other hand, would tell him almost daily the details of what I was learning from my dreams, meditations, and the grief groups and how I felt about it.

Because no one knew about Kevin's cause of death, I was exposed to people's reactions to those who died from drug involvement on a routine basis—or at least seemed that way. Everywhere around me, conversations about drug overdose and the opioid crisis and so-and-so being an addict cropped up. Before Kevin had died, I hadn't been close to the reality of it, but now I was.

Shortly before Kevin's toxicology results arrived, Scott Weiland from the band Stone Temple Pilots was found dead. Although the media didn't immediately give the cause of death, it was well known that Scott had struggled with addiction for a long time.

The day they made Scott's official cause of death public, a coworker came up to my desk to tell me about it. He and I had talked about music a lot in the past, so it wasn't unusual that he struck up this conversation, especially given the singer's notoriety and the recent story in the news.

"Did you hear Scott Weiland overdosed? No surprise there."

I sat frozen at my desk.

While Kevin's results hadn't been posted by that point, I was already terrified drugs could be involved given what was already found on the scene. This exchange with my coworker made me nauseous, thinking this would be how others would see Kevin if it was discovered he died from an overdose. I had nothing to suggest Kevin was addicted to anything, but any talk of death by drugs put me on edge.

When I didn't immediately respond, he knocked his knuckles on my desk and casually said, "Oh well. One more drug addict off the streets," implying that was a good thing and left me feeling like he just tossed a grenade in my lap. Every time something like this was said, I kept swallowing the bitterness that kept building.

*Is a person's worth determined by how they died? If drugs are involved, does that mean their life didn't matter? What about the families left behind—the person's mother, father, siblings, or spouse? What about their friends, nieces, nephews, and cousins? How can we dismiss the devastation of all these people because of how their loved one died? Where is the compassion? Doesn't their grief matter?*

I was beginning to see firsthand what stigma looked like.

◦ ◦ ◦

The pressure of hiding my shame came to a head several months later when I was in the middle of the training required to be a hospice volunteer. Separate from the parent grief group, I found myself drawn to wanting to have a deeper acceptance for the thing none of us could escape. I decided to try hospice volunteering, which seemed fitting as death was a subject I was consumed with; I thought I could do something useful with it. So, I began a ten-week certification training program that met every week for two hours.

There were twenty-five people in the training group, and one week, the discussion was about providing support to children who had lost a parent. The hospice grief program held breakout groups based on the kids' ages, which meant splitting off into separate rooms which increased the need for group facilitators.

"The opioid crisis has created a huge need for grief support. Children are losing their parents, and because of it, there has been an influx of kids ages three to seventeen who need support," the volunteer coordinator began.

I rubbed my sweaty palms on my pants under the table; the feeling of being exposed was never far away.

*Take slow deep breaths, Susan ...*

What happened next pulled the pin out of the grenade.

Out of nowhere I heard, "We all know what would help solve the opioid crisis, now don't we?"

I looked around the table to see who was talking and saw people sitting up straighter as if someone was going to say something very important. All the faces were all looking at one man sitting among us. There was silence as he looked around the table as if he knew someone would answer his seemingly obvious question.

When no one replied, he said plainly, "Family dinners. Families don't have meals together anymore." He dropped his pen onto his notepad and leaned back in his chair as if he just solved a complicated problem with an eloquent solution.

I felt all the air get sucked out of the room.

*I made family dinners! We sat together almost every night! I never missed a chance to talk to my boys about the important things!*

*We talked about drugs ...*

When Kevin was in middle school, talking about drugs was an easy conversation. Neither he nor any of his peers were doing anything other than sports at that age. When he was in high school, we had more ongoing discussions about drugs as certain trends surfaced. "Don't smoke marijuana," was always my stance, and my argument was that it was a gateway drug to harder stuff. We talked about inhalants and "huffing" when that was a trend in his mid-teens. I expressed my concern when he was in his early twenties when the drug 'Molly' was all over the news.

"Kev, you know about the drug called 'Molly' that goes around at music events, right?"

"Mom, they do Molly at all-night raves. I don't go to those. I go to jam band music festivals with names like the Frendly Gathering. I mean, come on, Mom. Their motto is 'There's no "i" in "frend."'"

We had open discussions about smoking marijuana. He was honest with me, telling me he was, in fact, smoking on a pretty regular basis. He was convinced it helped him relax and helped with his problem of falling asleep. His standard answer was "Pot is no big deal. No one has ever died from smoking pot."

Trouble began after high school when he went to college in Montreal and failed out after the first year.

His high school friends were all away at college, which made him feel like a failure. He became depressed and spent his time either at work or out with his new friends whom I didn't know. We had many discussions about making good choices, his increased dependency on smoking marijuana, and what his future plans were. I still have several apology letters from him saying he was going to "start over" and "make better choices."

When he was twenty-three years old, he told me he thought it was time for him to move out. He had a friend who was in California, working, who said he could get Kevin a job, and he could live with him if Kevin wanted.

"I can't be here anymore. I need a fresh start," Kevin told me one day. "I have a job and a place to live in California, and I want to go."

Hearing "I can't be here anymore" stung. "What do you mean?" I asked, feeling defensive as if I was being accused of failing him.

"Mom, I think you know. I need to break away from the people here."

I didn't know specifically who he was talking about, but deep down, I knew when he said "people," he didn't mean his family.

Some people have asked me if I ever regretted giving him my blessing, and my answer has always been "Not for one minute." I've always thought of it as the best gift I could have ever given him. He left for California knowing that I believed in him. I believed this would be a fresh start and that he would have a bright future.

All of the feelings I had been stuffing down came spilling out of me. Without awareness, I was standing with my hands holding onto the table for support, looking straight at him, pointing my finger wildly.

He had no idea the fury that was about to be unleashed until he realized he was the recipient of my glare. He abruptly broke eye contact and looked down, suddenly interested in thumbing the corners of his notepad.

"I MADE FAMILY DINNERS! WE SAT TOGETHER AS A FAMILY!"

Realizing I had just come out to the group about Kevin's cause of death, I held onto the table to keep myself from falling. My entire body betrayed me. There was nothing about me that was composed. I looked like a child having a temper tantrum complete with using my sleeve to wipe my nose and erase angry tears.

The fury of my adrenaline rush subsided as swiftly as it came. Suddenly, I felt more like a little girl who had just been told that nobody on the playground liked her.

"You have no right …" I said shaking, my cheeks hot with emotion. "… You have no right to say that …"

I closed my notebook, unclicked my pen, and stood up still glaring at him as I grabbed my purse. I made every effort to hold my head up as I walked out of the room and to the safety of my car where I climbed in, shut the door, and rested my now aching head on the steering wheel to fall apart all over again. The stigma was everywhere.

That confrontation happened on a regular Tuesday, but with complicated grief, every day had the potential of enduring some form of trauma. But the way trauma works is that you don't know it's coming.

●  ●  ●

Other than a brief stint in France, Matthew had been living in Montreal, Canada since graduating college. In 2016, the summer after Kevin died, he texted me to let us know he was moving out of his apartment and would be home the following week for a visit. I had been wishing he'd choose to come closer to home or at least move back to the United States, so I was hopeful he had made that decision. But when I asked him where he was moving to, he responded vaguely that he wasn't sure.

He arrived at our house somewhat pensive, and I thought having lunch in the backyard, just the two of us surrounded by nature, would soften his mood. He had grown his hair out, making blonde curls flick around his forehead and around the tops of his ears. The curls looked good on him, I thought, as I grabbed a potato chip.

Halfway through my sandwich, I started to wonder how this impromptu lunch was going. He was watching a cardinal that had just landed at the bird feeder, and I thought maybe my picnic in nature was doing what I'd hoped.

"I am going to South America," he blurted out.

"What?!" I said, taken aback, trying to remain somewhat composed. "For a vacation?"

"No, not a vacation." He said calmly.

"How long will you be there? Where will you stay?"

"Not sure how long—maybe six months. Maybe more. I don't know. I have an Airbnb booked in Argentina for the next couple of months. I might continue south after that," he said noncommittally.

As shocked as I was, this wasn't something completely out of his wheelhouse. He had been there on two other occasions, once being a semester abroad during college. He loved the culture, and he spoke fluent Spanish.

I had been worried about how much time he was spending alone while he continued to work remotely. Neither Tom nor I thought being so far away from home was a good idea, but he was adamant he was going. He hadn't shared much since Kevin had died, and other than the beautiful eulogy he wrote, Tom and I remained mostly in the dark as to what he was thinking or feeling.

I was always careful how I would ask him about his grief. I didn't want to push him into talking about his feelings if he didn't want to, and I also didn't want to make Kevin the only subject I talked about. My biggest fear was that I would come off sounding like I didn't care enough about Matthew and the fact that he was still here, still alive. It was an impossible situation. I had two narratives in my head.

*Ask him about his grief so he knows I care about his pain.*

*You'll give Matthew the wrong impression if you talk about Kevin too much.*

When I thought about him leaving, my rational brain tried to calm my fears.

*He is twenty-seven years old. He has traveled and lived outside of the USA for years. He will be okay.*

But a second later, I'd be thinking, *He has chosen to live on another continent and made it perfectly clear he does not want our help.*

He was choosing to flee, and I didn't want to leave my house—we were both trying to find our way, but I couldn't help but feel rejected and scared.

The following day, I watched Tom bring the car around to drive Matthew to the airport. Manny whined, presenting Matthew with his blue stuffed elephant as if to say *please don't go*. Matthew said goodbye to Manny with a quick pat on the head and climbed into the car, carrying a lone backpack, no international cell phone plan, and no timeframe of when he'd return.

Tripp took his place alongside me as I sobbed helplessly, watching the car roll down the driveway and up the street, taking another son out of my sight, out of my reach, and completely out of my control. Something as normal as him coming home for a visit and having lunch had turned into some new layer of grief I never saw coming.

A month after Matthew left, we were facing Kevin's birthday. Tom and I had made it through every first milestone and holiday since he had died, and the two biggies left were his birthday and the first anniversary of his death. We had decided that we would always take those two days off from work to spend them together doing something in honor of Kevin.

When he was alive, I had been dreading this birthday because it would be his twenty-sixth and he would no longer be on our health insurance policy. The smoke from the fires in California had been an issue for his asthma, which was a chronic problem that needed doctors visits and medication, but none of that mattered anymore.

On August 3, 2016, the day of his birthday, I set my alarm so I could be awake for his actual birth time, which was 5:14 a.m. Tom and I had our coffee while he mapped out a route to ride the motorcycle to the beach and a good place to stop for ice cream. We sipped our coffee in silence, off in our own thoughts, when I got up to go to Kev's room and do my morning meditation.

I sat down in my chair at the window and said, "Good morning, Kev. Happy birthday." I let the words sit, and I imagined the smile on his face in response. "Dad and I are going to the beach and are stopping for ice cream on the way home in honor of your special day." Again, I imagined his pleased expression, knowing we were doing something in his honor.

The Grateful Dead seeped into my awareness, and I felt it was from Kevin wanting to make our day a trifecta: the beach, ice cream, and listening to the Grateful Dead. Kevin knew I wasn't a Dead fan, but I said, "Okay, Kev. I'll try."

We arrived at Hampton Beach and walked onto the sand to lay out our stuff. After Tom and I walked along the water's edge, we sat on our towels, taking in the sights and sounds of the waves breaking and unrolling onto the sand.

We were both lost in our thoughts, staring at the ocean when I broke the silence and said, "Kev wanted us to listen to the Grateful Dead today."

He looked at me with a questioning expression.

"In meditation this morning, I was talking to him, and the Dead popped into my awareness. I think he wanted us to add that to our list of things to do today."

Tom was quiet then picked up his phone and started thumbing across his screen. He put it down between us as "Touch of Grey" by the Grateful Dead started to play. The gist of the lyrics was emotionally surviving when everything was wrong.

I couldn't help but wonder if Tom picked that song on purpose, trying to convince us both that we would get by—we would survive. But I wanted a lot more than just to survive; I wanted a purpose. I wanted my life to have some meaning. I wanted to stop hiding and to be able to shun society's notion that someone who died from an overdose deserved it for the poor choices they made, pointing fingers of blame on poor parenting, weakness, or lack of willpower. But I wasn't there yet.

I dug my toes in the sand, watching nearby kids making a sandcastle and, for a moment, wondered what they might be like as adults.

Thoughts of what my future looked like was unclear, but what did trickle in my consciousness was the idea, the possibility of letting the shame go for my future self.

*Someday I will openly grieve Kevin's death without feeling the added burden of stigma surrounding a bad way to die.*

*Chapter 11*

# One Bowl of Soup

*February 2017*

I had survived what they call in the grief world "the year of firsts." Daily meditating had helped open me up to a new way to communicate with Kevin, making me aware of signs and occasional dream visits from him. Spiritually, I was growing. Meditation was helping to keep him close, but I was still searching for something that would give my life on earth direction. At the same time, I continued to struggle in secret with the cause of death.

I had long since given up on thinking that someone else would have the directions for how to go on living my life and had come to accept the slow pace that my grief was insisting on. What may have helped the most was that Manny and Tripp seamlessly adapted to the new, slower pace of their lives, which taught me a lot about my own. Dogs naturally use all their senses to notice the details in their environment whether it is the smell of apples coming from the orchard across the street, the flag flapping in the wind, or the loud but muffled voices of a group of bicyclists whizzing by. Their ability to take in their surroundings had rubbed off on me, showing me how to live more presently, to notice details much like the way Kevin did.

But with that newfound sensitivity and observation, I became more aware of the injustices of the world. I was drawn to anyone who needed help, especially children, the elderly, and the homeless. There was some part of me still prone to that "magical thinking" I learned about in my grief group—that, somehow, I could have prevented Kevin's death if I had just done one thing differently. I couldn't help but continue to try to set it right even though I knew it wouldn't bring him back.

After finishing up at a doctor's appointment one afternoon, I stopped to pick up a pizza to take home for dinner. I pulled into the parking lot, and when I stepped out of my car, I noticed a young man about Kevin's age sitting on a bench just outside the restaurant. As I walked toward the door, he saw me and turned his head in the opposite direction, averting his face. I could see his brown curls sticking out from underneath the hood of a black sweatshirt. As I got closer, I could see the frayed cuffs of his bulky brown parka that half covered his hands wrapped around a backpack handle. I knew nothing about him but suddenly felt sad for him as I opened the door to the restaurant. My pizza wasn't ready, so I sat at a table near the window and pulled out my phone in an attempt to distract myself; but my thoughts were with this kid. I looked up from my phone and out the window to where he was sitting.

*Why did he deliberately turn his face away? Is he waiting for someone?*

I looked around to see if he might have had a friend getting some food. It was 4:00, so it was too early for the dinner crowd. I was the only one in the restaurant, and I started wondering about his parents.

*Do they know his whereabouts? Are they worried about him?*

A large man behind the counter looked at me. "Large cheese pizza?"

"Yes." I walked toward the counter and paid the bill. "Thanks," I said, picking up the hot box. The familiar smell reminded me of the hundreds of times I watched Kevin eating pizza with gusto. He always ate pizza until he was stuffed, and afterward, we all heard about how full he was as he grabbed "just one more slice." It didn't matter if it was homemade, frozen, or from a pizza parlor, he loved it all. Thinking of Kevin having one more piece put a smile on my face.

I walked outside, wishing I was taking it to Kevin as I passed the young man on my way to my car. Thoughts of Kevin filled my head as I turned the key and drove out of the parking lot. Waiting at a red light, I glanced over to the parking lot I had just left, and a thought came to me so spontaneously it startled me into the present.

*I can't give this pizza to Kevin, but I can give it to that kid.*

The rush hour traffic was starting, and I didn't make it through the light before it turned red again. When it finally turned green, I made a U-turn and pulled back into the parking lot and drove up to the bench that was now empty.

*He was just here.*

I looked all around the parking lot, but he was gone. I drove slowly past the restaurant window to see if he was now inside, but there still weren't any customers in there.

My opportunity to help had vanished with him, and my urge to help him felt linked to what I was supposed to learn from Kevin's death. Anything that got me closer to that level of enlightenment would give his death meaning. I pulled out of the parking lot feeling frustrated and sure I had missed an opportunity.

* * *

A few weeks later, on the 27th, my sister called me to see if I wanted to have lunch, and I agreed. I specifically remembered the day of the month because it was the 27th. A couple of months prior, I had a dream visit from Kevin telling me to pay attention to the number 27.

In the dream, Kevin appeared so clearly it was like he was back in his body, standing in front of me. I was lucid dreaming and knew I was being given an opportunity to get answers from him. In the dream, I also knew he was dead and just here for a quick visit with me; so I needed to hurry and ask the questions I had for him.

"Kevin, is that you?!" I asked excitedly.

He smiled and waved casually like it was only yesterday since I had seen him last and not the reality of being over a year since he had died. I sensed he was going to leave quickly and didn't waste more of our precious time together with obvious questions. After all, he was standing in front of me.

"How are we supposed to communicate with you?" I blurted out, but before he had a chance to reply, I rushed to the next specific question. "Where should Weezie send your cards?"

When my kids were growing up, my mother would always find a reason to send my kids cards to slip them a twenty-dollar bill and would often use random holidays as an excuse. She continued this tradition well into their twenties.

"Tell Weezie to send the cards to the house, and I will get them," he told me.

"And how are we going to know when messages are from you?" I asked next.

When Kevin was alive, he was known for writing sincere thank you cards dotted with humor. I knew he would continue to send us notes, but I needed to know how I would know they were from him.

Kevin simply said, "They will have the number 27 with it."

Our house number was 27, so this mailing system made perfect sense to me.

I woke up elated at having gleaned some information from him.

When the 27th came and it was time for me to meet my sister for lunch, I was hopeful something might come through from Kevin. But more than anything else, I was anxious about going out. It had been over a year since Kevin had died, but I was still leery of being out in public. The fear that someone I didn't know would ask those seemingly innocent questions—"Do you have kids? How old? How many?"—continued to burden me well before leaving the house.

On this day, I wanted to have lunch with my sister like old times, but to be safe, I chose a cafe where I wouldn't be likely to run into someone I knew. It was located in Nashua, a nearby city, and was known for roasting its coffee beans behind a glass wall next to the dining room so you could watch the process. The roasting machine gave off warmth and that fine coffee aroma, making the room cozy in the winter. My go-to for lunch was a toss-up between the stacked turkey, bacon, and avocado panini or the pastrami Reuben with sauerkraut and thousand island dressing. They also had great homemade soups with rolls and salads. Two of the exterior walls were large windows giving the room plenty of natural light and allowing a great view to people-watch on Main Street.

Lynne arrived at my house, and we drove together for the twenty-minute ride into the city. After feeding the meter a few quarters, we walked a few paces to the cafe and through the door. We were greeted by a waft of heat mingled with the aroma of roasting coffee beans. I had already had my regular morning coffee, but I decided I was going to treat myself to a latte. I rubbed my gloves together trying to rid the chill I had from just a few steps from the car. It was a bitterly cold morning.

I picked a table for two near the window, took my coat off, and sat down. The waitress walked over. "Hi. Can I get you ladies something to drink?"

"I'd like a latte, please."

"Club soda, please," Lynne requested.

"Great." She scribbled in her notepad. "I'll be back with your drinks." She offered us a smile and left. Lynne looked at the menu, and I realized I was more cold than hungry. I glanced at the soup of the day written on a chalkboard near the register. Maybe I would nix my usual.

"Soup of the Day: minestrone with a homemade dinner roll. That sounds nice and hot. Between that and my coffee, I think I might warm up by the time I'm done," I said, trying unsuccessfully to insert some levity.

"I know. It's freezing out," she said, rubbing her hands together simultaneously looking at the menu.

The waitress came back and placed our drinks down. "Do you ladies know what you would like to order?"

"I'd like the minestrone, please," I said.

"I'll have the house salad." Lynne gathered our menus and handed them to the waitress. "Okay. Wonderful. I'll get those put up for you." She scurried off.

I looked down at my latte and wrapped my hands around the warm ceramic cup, noticing how perfect the barista had made the flower swirl in the foam.

"It almost looks too pretty to drink," I said and looked at Lynne who was smiling at the effort someone had made to make it look so nice.

There was an awkward silence between us. We were both trying to have a normal lunch between sisters like we used to, but nothing was normal; and we both knew it. She broke the silence getting me up to date with the ongoing drama where she worked. I had missed out on the soap opera that was her office since Kevin had died, and it felt nice to be catching up, having light, familiar conversation.

I was facing the door while Lynne sat across from me with her back to it. Behind her was the last empty table in the room. I looked past her when I heard the bell jingle on the door and a man entered looking like he was wearing and carrying everything he owned. His heavy jacket and snow pants gave him a formidable look walking toward the empty table just behind Lynne.

*Don't stare. Give Lynne your attention.*

He shook his worn backpack to get the snow off it and put his duffle bag on the floor. He looked to be in his forties, but I suspected he might be younger than he looked. His skin was ruddy from being in the cold. I tapped my cell phone to get the time.

*It's noon. Has he been out all morning? Did he spend the night in the shelter? My God, he must be so tired all the time.*

His green knit hat covered most of his dirty blonde hair, and his black snow pants had red electrical tape preventing a six-inch tear from getting any bigger. He stood up slowly, holding the back of his chair so it didn't topple from the weight of his backpack and moved it to his seat, giving the impression he'd be right back. He turned, and with his head down, he proceeded to the bathroom.

Lynne was still talking; I injected a couple of appropriate nods, and she kept going. I was finding it hard to focus on what she was saying.

"Uh-huh," I said, glancing back at Lynne but keeping the empty table and his bags in my periphery.

As the man returned from the bathroom, he met my gaze for an instant, revealing spectacular green eyes before turning his attention to his chair, pulling it out, and placing his backpack on top of the duffle bag. I glanced around the room. Two teenagers sat across from each other, their thumbs frantically moving across their smartphone screens. An older man was reading the newspaper in between bites of his sandwich. A middle-aged woman tapped away on her laptop with a coffee mug inches from her right hand and white earbuds stuck in her ears. I looked back at the man who had his head down, sitting in the middle of the dining room, and I couldn't help wondering if he would have preferred a seat somewhere where he couldn't be surrounded by gazes and stares though no one seemed to be paying him any attention.

I knew the homeless tended to gather in this area due to the short-term housing and church missionary nearby. So, I made the assumption that he was homeless and in need of a break from the cold. His need to get warm outweighed the risk of possible humiliation of being asked to leave if he wasn't going to purchase anything. Unlike him, I had a home, ample food, and a place to sleep, but I knew the feeling of having a personal wound on display for other people to judge.

*What happened to him? What's his story?*

I wondered if he was anything like the homeless guy Kevin had befriended when he was at college in Montreal. Kevin had first seen a man sitting on the front lawn of a church he passed on the way to class. When the guy looked at him, Kevin being Kevin, gave him a nod and a wave. The guy acknowledged him with a "Whassup?" which was all the encouragement Kevin needed to start a conversation with him.

Apparently, the church lawn was a popular place for the area homeless to sleep without getting kicked out. Kevin told me he would often see the guy there, wave a greeting, and slip him a few bucks from time to time. On one particular evening, Kevin was walking past the church on his way to a friend's house, carrying some beer. When he passed the church lawn, he saw the man, stopped, and gave him one of his beers.

When he got to that point in the story, I said, "Kev, money is fine, but you probably shouldn't give him beer."

Giving me an immediate look of disappointment, he said "Mom, why would you automatically assume every homeless person is an alcoholic?" He went on to share the story of the man he had befriended and how he came to live on the street. Afterward, I was embarrassed that I had been so cavalier and judgmental. It was such a typical example of Kevin being his open-hearted self, and I wanted to be more like him.

Just then, the waitress came over to our table with our lunch. She placed the salad in front of Lynne and slowly put the hot soup in front of me.

"Is there anything else I can get you?" she asked.

"No, thanks," I said.

As she turned, she glanced at *the man* but walked past him greeting people at another table. "Hello. Can I get you …?"

*Did she know not to approach him because he wouldn't have any money?*

I couldn't decide if she was being kind to let him warm up or cruel for not asking if he'd at least like a glass of water. Lynne had moved on to talking about a movie when I abruptly stood up pushing my chair back, making a startling squeak as it scraped along the wood floor.

I reached down and lifted my untouched bowl of soup and took three strides toward *the man's* table and placed it down in front of him. It was so spontaneous I hadn't given any thought as to what I was going to say as I stood next to his table. I thought of Kevin and how, if he was there, he'd tell me that I was drawing attention to this man's plight.

*What would Kevin say?*

I knew Kevin would be more casual. I needed to smooth over my abrupt appearance that made his quiet presence more obvious than it already was.

"This was an extra from the kitchen, and I thought you might like to have it," was the unconvincing lie that came out of my mouth.

His green eyes looked up to meet my gaze for a second time and said, "I'm all set. Thanks."

"It's free," I said awkwardly and walked back to my table, grabbed my clean napkin and spoon, then placed them on his table. "Seriously, it's yours. Enjoy." I gave him my first sincere smile in a very long time.

My presentation certainly didn't come as naturally as it did for Kevin, and this man probably knew I was lying. I could feel nervous butterflies start to flutter as I waited for his response, hoping he would take my gesture the way it was intended. One corner of his mouth lifted ever so slightly, and he gave me a quick nod of thanks and picked up the spoon.

I knew what I did was not a big deal; I knew in the scheme of this man's life, it was a tiny gesture. One bowl of soup would not change his trajectory, but this moment changed mine. I had felt prompted to give him my soup, I acted on it, and he accepted it, which made me feel good. This felt like living based on my intuition and what was right for me, not based on prescribed ideas or expectations.

Hope and joy were two feelings that had been eluding me for so long I had forgotten what they felt like. It felt as if I'd just been given an answer to the question that had been torturing me: *Is my life just going to be something to endure?* I had been given an answer in my grief group, but it had been too vague to stick. No one else could answer that for me; the answer was mine to figure out.

I walked back to my table, smiling with my whole head, and joined my sister who had a look on her face like *What just happened?*

I looked at her, still smiling. "I know how I'm going to bring joy back into my life."

We spent the rest of lunch and the car ride home talking about what I was thinking I needed. Lynne was excited for me I think because it was the first time she had seen or heard me with any ounce of energy or feeling other than grief. I told her about the time I tried to give a pizza to that kid, but it didn't work out.

"I want to help people. I think that will be a big part of me feeling better," I said.

As we were talking, the idea morphed to what I wanted to share with others and that Manny and Tripp would be an important part of my plan.

*Why wouldn't they be?*

"I want to somehow include Manny and Tripp."

As soon as I said it out loud, I knew how.

*I'm gonna get them therapy dog certified.*

Having spent most of their lives training and traveling to shows, Manny and Tripp had countless situations where they were required to work among crowds and noise, which made the certification test a breeze for them. Both dogs were certified a couple of months later, but it was Manny who was a true natural at it.

Manny and I spent the next two years working as a therapy dog team for the hospice organization I had been connected with. His "job" was to be the greeter for children ages three to seventeen who had lost a parent. It fed my joy and purpose, sending my own ripple into motion.

Kids can go in and out of their grief, crying one minute, then playing the next. Manny gave the kids something to walk towards whether they wanted to pet him quietly, giving them a chance to look around the room without feeling awkward, or for the kids who wanted to see what tricks he could perform. Either way, Manny gave them brief respite. I remember one little boy who was so excited to tell me Manny reminded him of another dog he knew.

"Manny is such a good dog. I used to have a dog, but now I don't. Manny, you look just like my neighbor's dog!" he said in rapid succession.

I replied for Manny. "Is your neighbor's dog a golden retriever?"

"Um, I'm not sure ...," he thought. "She's a little smaller," he said while moving his hand halfway down Manny's leg. "She's black and white and has long hair. She's so cute, just like you!" he said while petting the top of Manny's head and dashed off to the art table.

I laughed, now understanding how Manny and this other dog were "similar" and it had nothing to do with their breed.

It was amazing to watch Manny fill a void in their young lives even if it was just for the time he was with them. He mattered to those kids, and they looked forward to seeing him. To be able to share him was therapy for me as well. It was a way for me to participate in my own healing, by helping them with theirs. It echoed what that group leader had said to me about why she was still going to group after all that time.

# Chapter 12

# Meet Me at the Horizon

*March 2017–October 2017*

It was easy to see the beneficial results once I found a purpose, a way to physically *be* in the world. It felt good to be sharing my dogs and my time to help make someone's day a bit easier or more pleasant. I felt Kevin's influence when I was making choices, could sense him in my meditations, and had received some undeniable signs. But was it my wishful thinking?

I was searching for people who, like me, wanted to know the connection with their child was still there and that we could still have a relationship—albeit in a new way. And in early 2017, I found them. They were in a grief support group called Helping Parents Heal (HPH). They hosted support group meetings on Facebook for parents and welcomed discussions of the afterlife. They had guest speakers who were grief specialists and researchers on the afterlife that discussed near-death experiences. The most popular meetings were ones that had evidential mediums (someone who could connect with a loved one in Spirit). It was also a place to share and celebrate the signs parents were receiving from their kids.

The more HPH online meetings I went to, the more I trusted my intuition, and the more confident I became that what I was receiving was coming from Kevin. I eventually decided I was ready to see a medium, but I didn't know who to go to. I had heard of people getting duped, and I couldn't bear the thought of having something like that happen to me with my deepest wound.

Each time I sat in Kevin's room to meditate, I'd light a candle, look out the west window, and say hello to Kevin to make sure he knew I was there. My next words were always "Please show me what I need to know today in a way that I can understand," and I would pay attention to what seemed to just fall into my lap; and one day it just happened. I was having lunch with my friend, Debbie, telling her about the "27 dream visit" when halfway through our burgers, she said, "I have a book that I think you are ready for."

The book, *The Shack* by Wm. Paul Young, arrived at my house two days later. All she said was that the story was about a father whose daughter had died and goes on a journey to understand his grief, and she thought it would resonate with me. So, I read the book. She was right. The message touched me deeply. Soon after I finished it, it had been made it into a movie, and when it came to our local theater, Debbie and I made plans to see it together. When I was online ordering my ticket a "coming soon" popup appeared on my screen that read "Gallery reading with Psychic Medium Necole Stephens."

"Wait, what?? That is nuts." I smiled, hearing my words, remembering that Kev used to say that phrase all the time. "Am I supposed to see her, Kev?"

*Please show me what I need to know today in a way that I can understand.*

I skimmed her bio.

She had lost her brother, her father, and her son within three years.

*She lost a son ...*

*She was pretty. Kevin liked pretty.*

*She was coming to Chunky's. Kevin saw many movies at Chunky's, so he'd know where to go.*

*She lost a son.*

*She's gone through child loss. She'd be honest with us.*

This medium had fallen into my lap.

I clicked "Buy Tickets" for Necole's gallery reading, which was scheduled for the upcoming weekend.

On Friday evening, Tom and I drove to Chunky's, and to our surprise, the entire room was already full thirty minutes before the event even started. It was open seating, and we found two seats together in the very back and waited nervously. We needn't have worried about sitting in the back because Necole moved around the room to be closer to the people she was reading for.

By the time it was over, Kevin hadn't come through, but we did witness a reading for the woman sitting next to us who was blown away by the current events Necole had brought through from the woman's deceased father. Watching the way Necole worked and the way the woman responded was fascinating and encouraging. Tom and I knew we wanted a private reading, so we booked one for three weeks later.

On the day of the reading, we arrived at Necole's house for our appointment at 1:00 p.m. Her long dark hair was pulled up into a ponytail. She looked comfortable in her black leggings and an oversized white button-down shirt with a large labradorite crystal perched on her ring finger.

We walked into her living room. There was a large couch and a comfortable oversized chair. Necole and I sat opposite sides of the couch with Tom an arm's reach away from me in the chair. She tucked her legs into a lotus position and started to give her an explanation of what to expect and asked if we had any questions. We did not.

"Feel free to record the audio on your phone," she offered.

Tom pulled up a voice memo on his iPhone, hit record, and put the phone on the coffee table. I had told Kevin before the reading that I didn't need any specific sign; I asked him just to show that he was still around me. But now that we were about to begin and the voice memo was recording, I started to think I should have asked him to be more specific.

She closed her eyes, took a deep breath, and said a short prayer aloud.

"We step forth to connect in Spirit with truth in love and welcome those who wish to do the same for the highest good of all involved. And so it is."

She opened her eyes but looked off to the side.

I glanced to see if there was something she was looking at, but I couldn't see anything. She was quiet for what seemed like an eternity, then began. "An older woman, a grandmother figure is here ..."

I instantly felt a pang of disappointment, but I kept a poker face. I loved my deceased grandmother, but I wanted to hear from Kevin.

"... She is bringing forth a young man. The male with her is younger. I don't feel like his passing was from this, but I feel lungs are involved; and I feel the need to clear my throat. I just want to keep clearing my throat and take a deep breath," she said, inhaling while tapping her sternum. She coughed and cleared her throat a few times.

We were instructed to give her "yes" or "no," but I offered, "He had bad asthma. He was clearing his throat all the time," feeling relief and surprise that he had made her feel his asthma.

"He is showing me a small piece of paper; it's very thin and belongs to you," she said looking at me. "Do you know what that is?" Without waiting for my reply, she continued. "It is very thin-like; you can see through it. It looks like parchment paper. He's showing me a tall dresser. It's in a tall dresser in the top drawer. A small piece of paper that has something pertinent on it. It's in the top drawer," she repeated. "It has black scroll font on it. It's see-through, thin paper," she said, rubbing her thumb against her fingers as if she were feeling it.

I had no idea what she was referring to and looked at Tom to see if it registered with him. Tom just shook his head.

I looked back to Necole and explained, "I went through his room thoroughly and didn't find anything like that, but I'll check again."

"It might not make sense now, so just write it down and make a star next to it to check when you go home. He is *insisting* that piece of paper is there," she said with a knowing smile.

I was feeling a bit discouraged with her insistence over the piece of paper in the top drawer. The description was so specific. I had gone through his room with a fine-tooth comb and didn't remember any kind of small, thin paper.

*Could I have thrown it away not knowing it would someday be important?*

I was glad to have the reading recorded so I could relisten to the details.

The hour went by, and we left with her bringing forth many specifics, even names that would not be searchable. Even Tom, who was skeptical, felt lighter when we left.

The first thing I did when I got home was search his room but to no avail. I got my notepad and read the details of how she described it.

*A small, thin piece of paper that was like parchment paper with something pertinent in black writing.*

I pulled up the recording Tom had transferred onto my phone, and I sat down and relistened. It was one of the first things she said so I didn't have to wait long to hear the whole description and where it was located. "It's in the top draw of the bedroom," she said, and I hit pause on the recording.

*She didn't give a specific bedroom. The tall dresser in the top drawer. Oh my God. He could mean the tall narrow dresser in MY bedroom!*

I ran into my room and pulled the knob on the top drawer of my tall, narrow dresser. I didn't have to rummage through any of the contents. Right on the top at the very edge was a fortune from a fortune cookie that I received four months prior. I liked what it said, and I kept it. The black font read, 'When I was young, I admired clever people, now that I am old, I admire kind people.' ~Abraham Joshua Heschel."

I held it up to the light coming from the window and could see through it. I rubbed it with my thumb against my fingers like Necole did and felt its slippery coating.

*Oh my God. It feels like parchment paper!*

I ran to the kitchen, opened the cabinet, pulled out a box of parchment paper, and pulled out a sheet to compare.

It was definitely parchment paper. I sat on the floor holding the small, thin piece of paper. The fortune did have "something pertinent on it," which is why I saved it. The words had spoken to me because it made me think how wonderful it is when I come across someone kind. I had forgotten I had even put it there, but Kevin knew it was there. I asked him to show me he was still with me, and he did.

That reading with Necole fed my need to learn more about unseen connections—with myself and Kevin. It prompted me to read dozens of books and take classes—classes called Understanding and Trusting Your Intuition, Dream Interpretation, and Grief Yoga. I was a sponge soaking up whatever brought me to a closer and better understanding of how to be closer to Kevin and find peace. I was also getting closer to starting a southern New Hampshire chapter of Helping Parents Heal in my area.

●●●

Somehow, time passed, and we were approaching the second anniversary of Kevin's death. Days before October 3, 2017, I found a poem called "Gone From My Sight" by Henry Van Dyke. In the poem, he describes himself standing on a shore with someone next to him. He is sad, telling the person with him about the woman he loves who has just died. He refers to her as a "beautiful ship" heading to a new destination, which the reader assumes is heaven. He watches her sail away from the seashore and him until the boat is a speck on the horizon. The poem ends with the message that people will say she is gone when they can no longer see the boat. The man on the shore knows that those who have gone before the woman are watching her arrive, and they cheer, "Here she comes!"

The last line of the poem is "And that is dying."

The poem left me imagining the horizon as a gateway from this life to the next. I knew that where the sun comes up to touch the ocean and the sky was the exact spot I wanted to be looking on the second anniversary of Kevin's death. That was where I wanted to be when I said hello to him on that day.

I was confident by then to know how to connect with him, and I was opened to receiving signs. I wanted to meet his second anniversary head-on and be awake for every minute of daylight. I had the idea of going to the ocean, watching the sunrise at the beach, and greeting the day and Kevin at the exact point where the sun rose along the Atlantic.

On the morning of his anniversary, October 3, 2017, I woke at 4:00 a.m., went to my computer, and shared a short tribute to him on my Facebook page. I picked a photo of four-year-old Kevin with his arm around our first puppy, Bailey. The last two lines of my post were written to Kevin:

"We will mark the second year of your passing at the Atlantic Ocean for sunrise. Meet you at the horizon, Kev."

The drive to Rye Beach was mostly quiet. I was lost in my own thoughts, thinking about how far we'd come with this new understanding of how to be together. I remembered with great detail the most recent dream visit I had with him.

In the dream, he and I were at an airport, standing face-to-face. He was giving me his best "I'm sorry" face. His shoulders were slumped forward, and his head was slightly tilted. But then it was like he suddenly decided he needed to take a stand and stop apologizing. He straightened himself up, met my eyes directly, and said, "Mom, I used bad judgment. I made a mistake."

I looked into the eyes I'd known for twenty-five years and said, "It's okay, Kev. Everyone makes mistakes," and he turned and left me standing there as he boarded a plane.

I have always had vivid dreams and have been recording them in a journal for some time. I had even taken a course on how to interpret your own dreams with dream shaman, Robert Moss. Kevin was asking for forgiveness—for me to forgive his mistake and for me to forgive myself. He wanted me to stop taking responsibility. I had suffered enough.

We arrived at the ocean at 6:00 a.m., and it was still dark as Tom parked the car alongside the road. This particular section of the coastline had large rocks all the way to the water's edge. I wondered if it was man-made to barricade the ocean from the street.

We each grabbed a towel from the backseat and used the flashlights on our phones to illuminate the rocks that were damp from the morning dew. We climbed the stairs and navigated a few rocks, moving us closer toward the water, spread out our towels, and sat down on the flat rocks.

"Is the tide coming in or out?" I asked, watching a small wave break on a rock.

"Coming in," Tom said.

The sky was indigo blue with just one thin cloud that was breaking up before our eyes. It was going to be a beautiful sunny day. A thin orange line was announcing the sun's arrival on top of the dark steel color of the water, and for a few seconds, the sky and the ocean were the same color. Against the water, the horizon was still orange, but above, it had turned yellow and the orange became a thicker line. We were surrounded by only sounds of seagulls squawking and the ebb and flow of the waves landing on the rocks.

"Sunrise is at 6:44, so we have another twenty minutes," Tom said, and we continued to sit in silence.

Nothing from the past was in my thoughts.

I sat focusing on the sun coming up and the seagulls dipping into the water, catching their breakfast. I was fully present when at 6:41 the tiny yellow line appeared and at 6:42 it became a small yellow mound and at 6:43 became a small yellow circle with its bottom covering the silver water.

I welcomed the day by saying good morning to Kevin in my mind, basking in the perfection of the moment, having our planned rendezvous. When we were content with the number of pictures we took to document the event, we stood up and walked back to the car. We pulled out of our parking spot and continued to drive alongside the ocean keeping an eye on the sun as it made its slow ascent into the sky. We passed a beach, and I wanted to get a picture of the sun that was now shining a streak of yellow along the water touching the sand.

"Pull over!" I said suddenly. "I want to get another picture of the sun with the beach in it."

Tom pulled into the parking lot, and I quickly jumped out of the car and took two pictures, put my phone in my pocket, and walked back to the car. We drove home both glad we went and discussed what our plans were for the rest of the day.

When we arrived home, I pulled out my phone and started going through the sunrise photos I had taken. I swiped my finger alongside the screen, smiling, thinking of our *meeting*. I stopped at the last two photos I took—the ones when I had asked Tom to pull over. The first one had a tiny orb-like yellow circle above the sun, and when I swiped to the second picture, there it was again but to the right of the sun sitting directly on top of the horizon.

"What is that?!" I asked Tom as I pushed my phone towards his face.

He put his fingers to my phone and spread the screen to make the yellow dot bigger. "I don't know," he said, staring at it.

"Lemme see it." I reached for my phone. "Do you think it is an orb?" I said looking at the enlarged dot. "Tom, I told Kev I'd meet him at the horizon. Look. I wrote it on my Facebook page," I said as if I needed to prove it. "Its position couldn't be more perfect. It's exactly on the horizon."

I went to my computer and started looking up what orbs look like to find out what exactly it was. The more I searched, the more hits I got, and the more deflated I became.

"It could be a lens flare from the camera," I said, the wind out of my sails.

"Why do you keep looking for what it actually is? Isn't the fact that it was on the horizon the important part?"

"Yeah, and the fact I suddenly had an urge for you to pull over and took only two pictures," I agreed suddenly feeling lighter again.

"It just matters that it happened when you told him you'd meet him there."

"You're right," I said. "I need to remember to be open to what I ask for. Even if it's not an orb, it is sitting on the horizon, which is where I told him I'd meet him. What more could I want?"

"Exactly."

Kevin had shown me exactly what I needed in a way I could understand.

# Chapter 13

# Press, Release

*October 2017*

Trusting that Kevin was guiding me gave me some peace, but the shame and feelings of judgment were always present, simmering just under the surface. For two years, the cause of his death had added even more weight to the grief blanket constantly wrapped around me, making every move and every decision a labored one.

I knew the answer to having joy within my new normal was to help others in some way, and with learning so much about the afterlife from the Helping Parents Heal online meetings, I felt strongly about spreading the word about the group to other grieving parents. I contacted the HPH co-founder to discuss the details of what I would need to do to become a facilitator in my area since the closest group was in New York, which was hours away. The first item of business was to secure a meeting place.

There was a historic barn in my town that had been renovated into a community center. It was an ideal location, so I dialed the town hall to see if they could help me secure an evening slot for my in-person meetings. I waited for someone to pick up on the other end.

"Hello. This is Jackie at the town hall. How can I help you?"

"Hi, Jackie. I am looking to see if the community center is available for a meeting place for a nonprofit grief group called Helping Parents Heal?"

"Oh, okay. Let me see ..."

"It would be once per month," I added.

Pause.

"So, it looks like the Boys Scout troop has recently given up their spot on the fourth Thursday of the month. That's the *only* evening available for the community center."

"The fourth Thursday of the month works perfectly," I said, relieved I had found something so easily and quickly.

"You have great timing," she said. "We rarely have availability, and when we do, the slots get scooped up fast. Today is your lucky day."

Tripp, who had been resting his head on my lap, lifted his chin and yawned. I winked at him knowing that the availability had nothing to do with luck; there was a greater power at work here.

"Wonderful. What is the fee?" I replied.

"As long as it's a nonprofit, it's free to town residents," she said. I could hear the happiness in her voice giving me the good news.

"Perfect," I said, and we planned a time for me to come in, fill out forms, and get the key.

Now that I had secured a location, I needed to get the word out. If the information about the HPH group could reach the masses, those who needed to come would be able to find us. My idea was to have a feature done on the new parent grief group in the local paper. I called the newspaper's office and spoke with Shelly, a reporter who liked the idea for the story and agreed to come to my home and interview me the following day.

Just before she arrived, I pulled out four photo boards we still had intact from the services and made a fresh pot of coffee. I was so grateful she was taking the time to write about the group and, essentially, helping me to help others.

She pulled into the driveway and parked, but when I looked out the window, I saw she was still sitting in the driver's seat with a look of apprehension. She had seen Manny and Tripp waiting at the screen door with stuffed toys in their mouths, whining in anticipation of having a guest to greet.

"They will calm down in about thirty seconds," I called to her, standing at the door alongside them. I was hoping she could see how funny they were being, but she just sat there nervously tucking her short brown hair behind her ears and adjusting her glasses. "They just want you to tell them you love their toy," I said jokingly through the screen trying to erase the serious look on her face.

When she didn't smile, I took that as my cue to call off the canine welcoming committee. I called the dogs into the kitchen and opened the sliding glass door to let them out into their play area outside.

"They're outside. Come on in." I hollered, walking back toward the screen door.

Grabbing her camera and notebook, she stepped out of the car and adjusted her white oxford before she walked into the house. She seemed more confident with the dogs outside. She rolled up her sleeves and walked over to the kitchen table to look at the picture boards.

"Would you like some coffee?" I offered.

"No, thank you," she said distractedly, pushing her thick eyeglasses further up her nose. "Do you mind if I take some pictures?"

"Not at all. Feel free."

I spent the next hour answering her questions, talking about Kevin, the Helping Parents Heal group, and the logistics of the new group I was forming. We talked about how in my small town alone, three kids recently died. I shared about how helpful the HPH group had been for me; that I felt that the group was going to be such a needed resource for our community; and I stressed that the group was open to all no matter their faith, background, or child's cause of death. Of equal emphasis was that the group did not replace therapy but was specifically a group for grieving parents to know they were not alone on this path and that we can continue the connection with our kids albeit in a different way.

She certainly wasn't warm, but she did give me her full attention and seemed genuinely interested in what I had to say. I had given her all the information she needed for the feature, and she had taken several photos. When she had stopped asking questions and there seemed to be a lull in the conversation, I assumed that our time had drawn to a close, and I stood up. Shelly hesitated but picked up her notepad and asked, "How did he die?"

I had almost made it without having to answer this question, hoping it wouldn't come up.

*Had I not been clear? The feature was about a new support group to help parents who have survived the trauma of outliving their child and to talk about how they were still connected to them. It was about helping parents learn that having a new kind of relationship with their child in spirit was possible.*

"The official cause of death was multiple drug intoxication. We don't know all of what happened that night other than he was drinking with friends at a party." Then, I quickly added, "I don't want that printed because I've not shared the cause of death with my family."

She nodded and said "Okay," and I was relieved that the discussion was over. I thanked her, and when she left, I gathered up the picture boards, put them away, and started making my lunch. Other than answering that last question, I thought the conversation had gone really well. I was excited to think of the impact this group would make on the community. I grabbed an apple from the fridge when I realized I had forgotten to ask Shelly when the story would be in the paper. Our first Helping Parents Heal meeting was scheduled in three weeks, and I was hoping the feature would run before then. I put my apple down and went to my computer to tap out a quick email.

*Hi Shelly,*

*Thank you again for agreeing to do this feature on Helping Parents Heal. I forgot to ask you when you thought it might be printed?*

*I've included a link to Kevin's eulogy (see below) just to give some idea as to what kind of a person Kevin was, not so much for the story but because I wanted to share it with you. :-)*

*Thank you again, Susan Lynch*

On some level, I thought sharing the eulogy might offset any feeling she might have had over how he died. I hit "send," walked back into the kitchen, and saw the dogs standing at the door. I slid it open, and they collectively bounded to the back door to see if our guest was still in the driveway.

"She left, guys." I grabbed my apple and my keys. Their attention shifted back to me, knowing that the sound of keys meant it was time for our walk.

They hustled to the door to the basement stairs, waiting for me to open it.

"Ready?" I asked, opening the door.

They replied "yes" by racing each other down the stairs to get to the truck parked in the garage.

*This is turning into a very good day.*

I loaded the dogs into the truck and drove out of my driveway to head to one of my favorite trails to walk.

Driving through town, I reached to turn the radio station and heard the Grateful Dead's song "Bertha" start to play. I turned the volume up loud and started bobbing my head and laughed out loud thinking about Kevin's friend Ryan saying "Kevin loved a good Bertha" when I had asked Ryan if Kevin had liked the song I had grown to love.

I glanced at the dogs in the rearview mirror. They were looking at me with their ears up like they might be enjoying this Dead song, too.

"Anymoooore mmmm hmmm," I sang, bobbing my head as we drove through town.

The entrance of my favorite trail starts with a steep hill into the woods and has a stream halfway up so the dogs can cool off and I can catch my breath. At the top of the hill, the trail opens up to two thirty-acre grassy fields surrounded by classic New England stone walls. Branching off the fields are various hiking trails going off further into the woods.

I always visit the huge beech tree tucked in the woods alongside a narrow trail and stand under it. On a sunny day, the sun makes the leaves the prettiest color lime green and although beautiful, it also holds deep meaning I've always been drawn to. My friend, Mirium, who delves deep into earthy energies, once told me that the magic of the beech tree is to identify and heal some of our deepest pains if and when we are ready. The beech's bark is very thin and always bears its scars but continues with life, not hiding its sensitive qualities from anyone. I always loved the idea of standing in solidarity alongside something beautiful that had scars and to stand among its energy hoping to get some healing from my pain.

I pulled into the dirt turnoff at the trailhead, parked my car, and pulled out my cell phone to text Tom. I had forgotten to let him know how well it went with Shelly. There on my screen was an email notification. She had already replied to my email.

*I'll bet she was as moved as everyone else who read the eulogy. I hope she's gonna tell me the feature will be coming out in next week's edition.*

I tapped on the email and read:

*Susan,*

*I have a great deal of respect for what you're doing, but not giving the cause of death would mean a big and unacceptable hole in the story. Without that fact, all I can do is run your photo with information about the support group and your contact information in the caption.*

*Shelly*

"What??" I said out loud, suddenly confused.

*Wait, that can't be. I didn't read that right.*

I read it again slowly, but my eyes didn't move past the word *unacceptable.*

"Unaccep ..." I started to say the word out loud, but it only half came out like it was lodged in my throat, choking me.

*Unacceptable? My choice not to share my son's cause of death is unacceptable to you?*

I looked back at the email. The confusion dissipated, and rage took over.

*Where was the "Dear Susan" part? Where was the "I'm sorry"?*

I had invited her into my home and placed my trust in her. I opened up for the first time to a stranger, thinking that she would help me. *Did she even read the eulogy? Did she delete it?*

The dogs moved in their crates, and I looked in my rearview mirror to see them both sitting up looking at me. I tossed my phone on the passenger seat, got out of my car, and let the dogs out. My adrenaline and fury had reached a fever pitch, and I needed to move my body. The three of us started up the hill.

*How dare you ... How dare you judge what I do to protect my heart.*

The rage came out in angry tears as I headed up the hill.

*She wanted that one fucking salacious detail of how he died.*

By the time I reached the top of the hill, I was so filled with bitterness I could practically taste the bile in my mouth. We were the only ones there, so we kept walking down the lane that divided the two fields, heading for the wooden bench at the edge of the stone wall. When we reached the bench, I pointed to the ground, signaling the dogs to lie down. I needed to collect myself, get my anger in check, but when I put my hands on the bench, I felt all my pain rush to the surface. I pushed against the bench as hard as I could and wailed.

When the tears relented, the anger rose again, and I started to pace and kicked a rock. When it only rolled a couple of feet, I picked it up and hurled it, releasing a primal scream. I stood shaking, my back toward the dogs.

I was afraid of how angry I was.

The dogs had seen me through so much emotional upheaval, but they'd never seen me like this. I turned to see them lying in a sphinx position, ready to pop up at a moment's notice. Their look of concern softened only slightly when I signaled for them to come to me.

"It's okay," I said, attempting to reassure the three of us as we continued our walk. They walked closely alongside me to the edge of the field, and we headed into the woods. "This way," I said and changed direction to walk toward the big beech tree.

"Down," I said softly as we reached the beech and they laid down, each resting on their hip, looking a little more relaxed.

*I need to think.*

I looked up at the bright green canopy above me. A couple of branches extended over the trail like a roof over the three of us. For a brief moment, I imagined those sweeping branches curling as though they were arms and swooping me up. I needed to be held.

I placed my hands against the smooth gray bark.

*Please heal my pain. I don't want to be an emotional loose cannon anymore.*

I ran my finger along the heart surrounding initials that someone had carved long before I had discovered the tree.

"Why am I so mad?" I asked the Universe, desperately wanting an answer, and leaned in, pressing my forehead to the cold bark.

*I need peace.*

I was tired of battling with the secrecy and shame from the stigma surrounding Kevin's cause of death. I closed my eyes. Suddenly, the image of Kevin's arrest photo on the front page of the newspaper flashed into my mind.

Slowly, I pushed myself away from the tree and let the revelation sink in. I knew from meditating on particular questions that this was how the answers came to me. Images flashing into my mind like the way a new idea pops into consciousness, so I knew this image—these flashes—were something to explore. There was some connection here.

He had been arrested during his senior year in high school for underage drinking, which made the front page of a different local newspaper along with his mug shot. Our extended family lived outside of the paper's circulation area, and Kevin, who was both embarrassed and remorseful of his actions, had asked me not to tell the extended family. He especially didn't want his grandparents to think badly of him, so we agreed to keep it quiet.

Tom, Kevin, and I had a long discussion about making poor choices and the consequences that could affect his health and his future. He had done his community service, paid the fine, and wrote us a three-page apology letter taking full responsibility for his actions with a promise he would make better choices in the future. Today that letter is neatly folded and tucked away in my drawer.

During that time, keeping Kevin's arrest hidden from my parents was stressful. One time his community service coincided with his grandparents' visit, and when they asked where he was, I felt as if I had a sign over my head saying he was in trouble with the police. Both Kevin and I were nervous they'd somehow find out, but they never did, and we successfully got past that time.

I remembered all the emotions of hiding the truth, feeling even back then that I had somehow slipped up with my parenting. I recalled the day I passed two mothers of kids in Kevin's class walking into the convenience store in the center of town. The moment I saw them, I started rummaging through my purse to avert my face, to avoid seeing their stares, and to drown out any real or imagined whispers of what they might be saying about me as a mother.

I had felt Tom and I had gotten our point across, and Kevin knew he was wrong and believed that was enough. He was a teenager that had a lapse in judgment. I didn't want to make him more ashamed by telling his grandparents, and here I was years later, ashamed about another newspaper story but this time over wanting to print his fatal mistake. This time, the newspaper needed my permission to print, and this time, I could choose to handle the situation differently.

*Kevin admitted he had made a mistake. He wanted me to forgive myself and let go of the responsibility of it all. Do I want to continue to hide, or do I honor what he would want for me?*

I recalled watching a TED Talk by Brené Brown on listening to shame and about being vulnerable. According to her research, shame needs secrecy, silence, and judgment to thrive. All these years I had kept quiet, I was unknowingly feeding my shame.

I called the dogs to me and started to pet them, feeling a new sense of calm at having just discovered the source of my pain. From all the work I had done processing my grief, I knew that figuring out the source for any emotion was a big first step. The second step was to figure out how I was going to deal with it. The obvious solution came to me just as quickly.

*I have a choice. I can continue hiding or I can be open and let go of the shame.*

Back at the beech tree, I placed my palms against it.

*Thank you.*

I felt as if a weight had been lifted off me, and I had an overwhelming sense of gratitude for all the moments of tenderness and care Manny and Tripp had given me. Kneeling down to be face-to-face with them, I scratched under their chins, and they brought their muzzles closer to me. I marveled at the fact they never had a way of knowing when I would be "better," and yet they never wavered in their dedication to me.

"You guys have seen me through so much." I buried my face between them, expressing my gratitude with soft whispers in their ears. "I love you. I love you. I love you."

Lifting my head, I read their expressions: *We love you, too.*

I wiped my cheeks with the backs of my hands, took a deep breath, and stood up exhaling fully.

"No more hiding," I said to all who were listening— the dogs, Kevin, the Beech tree, the Universe, and myself. I shivered upon hearing my declaration, leaving the leaden blanket at the base of the tree.

"Let's go, guys," I said, and the dogs sprang up to join me. I walked back to the truck, feeling the lightest I had felt in a very long time.

Driving home, my mind was filled with thoughts of Tom, what his reaction would be to Shelly's email, and my decision to finally come out with the secret. I pulled into the garage, walked up the basement stairs to the kitchen, and gave each dog a biscuit that they promptly took to their respective beds to eat. I briefly wondered if they thought taking care of me was hard work. I hadn't even taken my coat off when I walked straight to Tom's office and quietly cracked the door in case he was on a call.

Peeking my head in drew his attention.

"I need to talk to you when you get a few minutes. No emergency," I added. It was now our custom to do what we could to avoid unnecessarily alarming each other. Five minutes later, he walked into the kitchen and stood at the kitchen island as I poured hot water over my teabag.

Even though I had said no emergency, he had a look of concern etched on his face. "What's up?" he said cautiously.

When I started to speak, it all just poured out of me—the email, my unraveling on the walk, and my revelation. I handed him my phone to show him Shelly's email and watched his face turn to a scowl as he read it. He tossed my phone on the island when he was done as if to distance himself from Shelly's words.

"I am ready to tell everyone how Kevin died," I said calmly and with certainty. He knew what a big deal this was for me, and his expression softened.

Before he had a chance to respond, I continued. "I want to let you know how grateful I am that even though you didn't feel the same way, you agreed to let me keep this private as long as I needed to."

I wrapped my hands around the warm mug and watched the steam come up, giving him a chance to respond.

"I wanted you to feel that you were ready to tell people," Tom said.

Upon hearing him say those words, I couldn't have felt more loved or understood.

Although he hadn't felt the same way, he respected my need to keep quiet. Never once, had I considered how hard it must have been for him to not be able to talk to his brothers or his parents about the circumstances surrounding Kevin's death. Just then I realized the magnitude of what I had asked and how he had done it for me without hesitation.

My friend and lover of more than thirty years who stood across from me at the small kitchen island could still make my heart expand to the point of bursting. I walked around the island and wrapped my arms around him with fresh tears streaming as we held each other. For the second time that day, I felt an overwhelming sense of gratitude.

My fury towards Shelly had dissipated with my enlightenment and my conversation with Tom. I felt calm enough to respond to her earlier email. I went to my computer and typed out my response:

*Hi Shelly,*

*I am sorry that I did not express the meaning of the group clearly. The story is about a new group for grieving parents, not about how my son died. Measuring the degree of loss based on the cause of a child's death happens all the time and is something I do not want to perpetuate. I am saddened you feel that it is necessary to include it for this story to be complete.*

*In any event, I appreciate you taking the time to interview me. Running a photo with the Helping Parents Heal dates, time, location, and contact information would be greatly appreciated.*

*Regards,*
*Susan Lynch*

・ ● ●

The day I went to my parents' house to tell them, they quietly sat at the kitchen table, their hands folded in their laps, listening to me as I let it all out. When I was done dropping my grenade, my dad looked at me. His voice, his face, his whole body was soft and gentle. "It doesn't change anything.

It doesn't change how we feel about Kevin. We will always love and miss him."

My mother had tears running down her face and nodded in agreement. "Nothing could ever change how we feel about Kevin."

Shelly's email had stirred up years of bitterness and anger that had been waiting to be addressed. Once I recognized it had roots in another experience, I realized it had reappeared to teach me. I will always give a nod to Shelly for being part of my healing process. Her role wasn't to help me spread the word about the HPH group; her role was to force me to face the source of my anger, defensiveness, and shame and to release it once and for all.

I went forward with being an affiliate leader for the Helping Parents Heal support group for two years before turning it over to a couple of moms who saw the value and wanted it to continue. Like the other parent who had continued to attend meetings to offer support, I, too, found that by helping others I was helping myself.

# Chapter 14

# Whoops-a-Daisies

*October 2017–April 2018*

I spent the month of October 2017 finally opening up to friends and family about Kevin's cause of death. Although they were saddened that I had taken on the burden for so long, they all expressed nothing but love and compassion to both Kevin and me. After two years, I was finally sharing what I knew, and although it was difficult to retell the story to each of them, it ended up being a big part of my healing.

During that time, I noticed Tripp was drinking more water than usual. I knew exactly what that meant. I also knew I wasn't ready for what was coming.

When Tripp was a year old, he had tested positive for Lyme disease. Further testing showed part of his kidneys were damaged. At the time, the specialist at Tufts veterinary hospital said the treatment would be determined by his lab work and symptoms. He was in the very early stages of kidney disease and only needed to have blood and urine checked yearly until he started showing signs of decline. One of the first signs was increased water intake.

When I saw he was taking in more water than usual, I took him for updated labs, and they came back showing a significant decline from his previous ones. His kidney disease had progressed. The last four months of his life would become frequent trips to the vet for blood draws, urinalysis, changing his meds, increasing his meds, and adjusting his diet.

Every test result felt like a sucker punch. On paper, he was rapidly declining, but he still was acting silly, showing us his favorite pink monkey, and eating well, which gave me a false sense of hope. By January, he was sleeping for most of the day and didn't have the energy for walks. With each passing day, I was becoming increasingly anxious over losing him.

By then, it was clear he could only handle us going for a "walk" around our two-acre yard. When he was healthy, he would follow me on the trails, but these yard walks were about me following him. While preparing my lunch one afternoon, a fork slipped from my hand and dropped to the floor, startling him awake. For just a moment his face was that of healthy Tripp, ears up and alert as if he had forgotten he was sick. He went to stand up, and I could see it took a little effort; but then he gained some pep as he went to the backdoor lifting my spirits.

*It's not time. He's not ready. I am not ready.*

I took him out for a walk around the yard, and when we came in, I called the renal specialist at Tufts. I wanted to give her an update with the hope that maybe there was something more we could do for him. She reaffirmed what I already knew, saying she was sorry and that other than enjoying the time we had left, there was nothing else to try. We talked briefly about euthanasia and when the right time would be. She gave me the same advice I'd given others when I worked at the animal hospital. "You'll know when it's time."

A few days after that phone call, I was in Kevin's room with the dogs for my morning meditation. During that meditation, I had drawn a series of images; two, in particular, were very specific. One was a series of paw prints in a walking pattern on wet sand, and the other was of an airplane.

I often use meditation drawings or things I write as guidance to help untangle my thoughts and emotions or to answer questions. But these images seemed more literal and symbolic—like a message for me to interpret. After a moment, the first part came to me. Although Tripp and I were always together, there weren't any human footprints next to the paw prints. While I knew his death was coming, the pawprints were before the airplane image. I was getting a heads up that he would pass right before we were to leave for our thirtieth anniversary vacation we had planned back to Costa Rica.

I told Tom how I felt, telling him I couldn't get on the plane; I couldn't leave Tripp. As the days got closer to our scheduled departure, the symbols proved true. Just days before our flight, Tripp took a dramatic turn.

We offered him cooked chicken, steak, and ice cream, but they were met with only mild interest. Four days before we were to get on the plane, he refused all food and water and became restless during the night. Tom lifted him into our bed, and he settled for a few hours but woke up panting heavily, visibly uncomfortable. As soon as my veterinarian's office opened the next morning, I called. It was time.

On the way to the vet's office, my thoughts wandered. I was surprised that even with all the advanced warnings, I felt completely unprepared for his death. I hadn't been able to talk to people about it. Saying how I felt out loud felt like I was minimizing Kevin's death by feeling Tripp's so deeply. I shared my anguish with Tom who said, "Tripp is funny. He's like the canine version of Kevin."

I looked at him from the passenger seat, surprised to hear him say that. I never realized Tom had felt the same way.

"I think so, too. He reminds me so much of Kevin."

He continued. "He's only six years old. He's dying in the prime of his life, just like Kevin. There is some commonality here."

There was silence between us as I let Tom's words sink in. I hadn't made that connection, but it made perfect sense.

*How am I going to manage without Tripp's support?*

He was my reset button on a bad day. I thought about how far I had come since Kevin's death because of him. When I thought of his kidney disease and how it could have progressed much faster, I realized he had stayed around just long enough to make sure I could stand on my own before he went Home.

We pulled into the parking lot, and I pulled some fresh tissues out of the box and wiped my eyes. "Kev, please make sure you are there to help Tripp cross over."

We slowly walked with Tripp into the hospital, and my favorite technician came out to usher us into a room. She hugged me, kissed Tripp on the head, and blew Tom a kiss as she walked back out to get Dr. Churchill.

Dr. Churchill walked into the room, wiping tears of her own, and hugged us both. She said we could take as much time as we needed to say goodbye and just crack the door open when we were ready. She handed me a box of tissues and gave me the answer to the question that wasn't spoken but was written on my face.

"You're doing the right thing." She quietly closed the door behind her.

Tom said his goodbyes, and I asked him if he would give us a few minutes alone. He nodded and left the room.

I stroked Tripp's fur and rubbed his ear in the way he liked. I reminded him of the conversation we had the day before about all the fun he would have playing with Kevin. I reminded Kevin: "Please make sure you help him cross over and take care of him until I get there." I sat on the blanket next to Tripp, sobbing over the image of them playing together without me. Tripp had sensed Tom was back in the room and opened his eyes to look at us one final time. Tom wiped his cheeks with the back of his hand. "Are you ready?" he sniffed. I gave a small nod, indicating he could crack the door.

Dr. Churchill did what had to be done and slipped out of the room. I held his head in my lap gently stroking the face that had given me so much. "I will miss you," I whispered. Sitting in silence, we waited as his spirit left to join Kevin.

That was a Tuesday. When we got home Manny was out of sorts looking for Tripp around the house, which made me worry about his grief, too.

Tom and I were scheduled to leave for our wedding anniversary vacation three days later. *How is Manny going to handle us leaving, too?*

We had originally planned for both dogs to stay with our friends, Milly and Stew, while we were gone. Milly adored my dogs, and her two dogs were best buddies with both Manny and Tripp. We had discussed canceling, but Tom convinced me that spending some time by the ocean away from the freezing temps and snow might help to soothe my aching heart.

"Manny will have Milly's dogs to play with. You know they are all friends," Tom said. Not knowing what else to do, I had agreed, but as I boarded the plane, I couldn't have felt more fragile. Once again, I found myself waiting for a sign from Kevin, but this time it was to let me know he was with Tripp.

My carry-on bag consisted of comfort items—a small Ziploc of Tripp's fur; a greeting card with a pink frosted donut on the front that read "*Donut Panic*," and when you opened it, the card had the words "*it will all be okay*;" and one of Kevin's festival bracelets. I had found the card at a store when I was having a particularly bad day. The silliness of it resonated with me, and I thought it would be a card that Kevin would send me to give me some reassurance; so I bought it.

When we booked the trip, Tom and I discussed how we felt about going back to Costa Rica where we last saw Kevin alive. We both knew parts of the trip might be hard but agreed that we wanted to be surrounded by the breathtaking scenery, animals, and the Pura Vida vibe that deeply resonated with us. Although we had discussed some possible triggers, one I hadn't considered was to be in the San Jose airport again. The image of Kevin walking away to board his flight back to California flooded my thoughts. I felt the familiar lump in my throat thinking we were standing in the exact same gate area when we had unknowingly said goodbye to Kevin for the last time.

Tom gave me a knowing look as if he was reading my mind.

"It's okay. I'm just thinking of Kevin," I said and wiped the tear that had made its way down my cheek.

"Me, too," he said, and we left to head to the rental car counter.

The drive was two hours to our villa, which was an additional hour south of where we had stayed with our family. The villa was perched on the side of a mountain, which was a precarious thirty-minute drive up a steep, winding dirt road, but once we arrived, its view of the Pacific didn't disappoint. The entire ocean-facing wall was a series of four sliding glass doors and steps away from an infinity-edged, saltwater pool overlooking Costa Ballena (Whale Coast) of the Pacific Ocean. At low tide, we had an excellent view of the sand formation called The Whale's Tail, a fin-shaped sandbar made by converging currents that deposit sand on top of rock formations.

I was glad we were back in Costa Rica. Tom was right. Being surrounded by the beauty of the country, the ocean, and the sun would be a balm for my heart. I unpacked my bags, put the Ziploc of Tripp's fur under my pillow, and went downstairs to place the Donut Panic card on the coffee table. I wanted it to be in a place where I would see it multiple times per day as a reminder that *it will all be okay.*

Each morning I went out onto the balcony off my bedroom to be greeted with a steady lull of insects chirping and yellow-throated toucans gathering on the limbs of a single tree in the distance. I listened as they called out to others of their species who had yet to arrive. Every morning, they came one by one, and within an hour, the tree was covered with toucans.

About halfway through our stay, instead of being able to relax my thoughts for quiet meditation, my thoughts kept drifting to Tripp. It had been almost a week since he had passed, and I hadn't received any sign letting me know he was with Kevin. Kevin had been such a good communicator thus far so I was starting to get anxious.

*Maybe I should just ask for a specific sign so I won't miss it?*

I had learned from a medium that this was possible. "Ask for something specific, and the most important thing is to be open as to how you receive the sign you ask for."

I had tried this on a few occasions to test it, choosing something that just popped into my head. One time, I asked Kevin to show me a gold ring, and I gave him one day to do it. I wasn't expecting a gold ring to be given to me, but I wanted to see how it would show up. Later that day, I was thumbing through a magazine while in the waiting room of my doctor's office when I saw an ad for the board game Monopoly. The picture in the ad was a close-up of the gold diamond ring square on Luxury Tax.

*What should I ask for?*

Instantly, the image of a daisy popped into my mind.

*Oh. Great. I am in Costa Rica. Where am I gonna see a daisy? Why couldn't I have thought of a tropical flower?*

Daisies were one of my favorite flowers and a perfect one to represent Tripp, knowing the flower's message is one of hope and renewal. To offset the odds of seeing one in the middle of the tropics, I asked Kevin to show me a daisy in any way, shape, or form. I was getting anxious and wanted to make sure he had Tripp with him. Although I was feeling confident he would come through with my request, my mothering habits were hard to break, and I repeated myself in case he wasn't paying attention.

"Good luck, Kevin, and don't forget … I need a daisy from you."

I walked downstairs and joined Tom for coffee and made plans for the day, knowing Kevin would somehow handle the rest.

We had already gone kayaking through the mangroves and took a two-hour hike up a mountainside to a lagoon with a waterfall. Today's agenda was to relax at the beach and stop for fish tacos on the way back to the villa. Tom packed the cooler while I loaded the SUV with towels, sunblock, his Kindle, and my book. As I walked past the coffee table on my way out to the car, I gave the Donut Panic card a nod saying, "I know" and walked out the door.

We arrived at the beach and set up our chairs in the shade under some palm trees. The typical temperature during the day was well into the 90s when you were off the mountain, and by mid-day when the fog was gone, the sun was unrelenting. I pushed my beach chair into the sand and reached for my book that had turned out to be a fun beach read. Tom set up his chair, then turned to me.

"I'm going in the water," he said. "You coming?"

"Not yet. I want to finish this chapter."

I watched him jog on his tiptoes across the hot sand and dive headfirst into a huge wave that was cresting. I found myself holding my breath for a couple of seconds before I saw his head pop up, facing the horizon, looking for another. The only other people at this beach were a handful of surfers spread out in the water, lying on their boards, waiting for the next wave to rise.

Tom started jogging back to our chairs, so I was free to stop worrying about possible riptides and get back to my book.

In the last scene of the last chapter, the main character, in a clumsy rush, slipped, holding a bunch of gifts, and called out sarcastically, "Whoops-a-daisy!" I chuckled at her, then closed the book. I was now hot and wanted to go for a swim.

*Wait ...*

I stopped myself from getting up. I reached for the book, reopened it, and read the last line again.

"Whoops-a daisy!"

*This daisy is in written form.*

"Oh my God. I asked for *a daisy!*"

I began to laugh.

Tom looked up from his Kindle to see what I was laughing about, and I handed him the book and pointed to the line. "I asked Kevin for a daisy to let me know he had Tripp," I said triumphantly.

He looked to where I was pointing and looked at me. "Holy shit," he said.

"I know! Right?!" I said, laughing. I looked up to the sky and said, "Thanks, Kev!!"

The next day, we packed up and drove back to the San Jose airport. This time at the airport, there weren't any tears. I was still feeling the magic over my *Whoops-a-daisy* and kept thinking how clever his delivery was.

Our trip home had included a stopover in Miami where we had to go through customs, and the line we had to wait in was ridiculously long. I was starting to get anxious that we might miss our connecting flight when a large woman in line directly in front of us turned around, facing me wearing a blue t-shirt with daisies on the front. My mood instantly shifted, knowing somehow Kevin would see to it we wouldn't miss our flight (and we didn't).

When we arrived home, I went to the post office to collect my mail and thumbed through the stack. In the pile was a sympathy card from Dr. Churchill. When I opened it, I gasped at the single daisy on the front of the card. The following day I saw a children's book with a little girl eating a frosted donut (of all things) with a daisy on her shirt. The daisies' signs continued to show up for seven consecutive days, which I was certain translated to *Hi, Mom! Don't worry. I've got Tripp!*

●　●　●

In April of 2018, two months after returning from Costa Rica, I was back on an airplane, but this time, I was alone. The founding members of Helping Parents Heal had planned a three-day conference in Scottsdale, Arizona. When I had originally opened the email announcing the registration was open, I read "Please join us for a joyful and uplifting weekend!"

These were not words I would expect to describe a group of parents whose connection was that their kids had died, but I knew from the meetings, this group was special. A large part of Helping Parents Heal was about sharing signs and messages from our kids, validating that they were still with us.

Tom didn't want to go to the conference but had encouraged me to go. I didn't have an issue with being there alone; my only reluctance was the flight. I don't like to fly by myself and wanted something that would make me feel more comfortable, so I thought to book seat number 27, knowing that Kevin would be with me.

I was scheduled to have a reading from a spiritual medium and had given Kevin plenty of reminders in the weeks leading up to the conference. There were over a dozen mediums to choose from, and since I didn't know any of them, I let my intuition choose Tina Powers.

The conference was booked to capacity with five hundred parents who had had one or multiple children die. The welcome dinner was on Friday night, and after the meal and listening to the last speaker, I headed back to my room.

My reading with Tina was scheduled the next morning at 10:00 a.m., and I wanted to make sure I was well-rested.

I got off the elevator and walked down the hallway thinking how strange it was for me to be without either Tom or the dogs. I had traveled without a human companion when showing dogs, but I had never stayed completely alone, which got me thinking of Tripp.

I put the key card up to the lock and pushed the handle down when it beeped. I got into my pajamas, sat on the bed, and started talking to Kevin to remind him of our meeting with Tina.

"Okay, Kev. The reading with Tina is tomorrow morning at 10:00. Please make sure you bring Tripp with you. We are in Scottsdale, Arizona. At the Embassy Suite hotel. Tina and I will be in room 125. Please don't forget to bring Tripp. I'm really missing him."

I realized I sounded like I had just sent him a bunch of logistical text messages and that I only mentioned that I wanted to see Tripp.

"Kev, you know I want you to show up, too," I said awkwardly trying to cover the fact I had neglected to mention it.

"Kevin, please show up for our meeting with Tina. I love you so much. I'll see you in the morning, okay?" I blew him a kiss, turned off the light and slipped under the covers.

At 9:50 a.m. the next morning, I stood in the hallway outside room 125. I knew mediums usually sit in quiet meditation before readings so I didn't want to knock and disturb any clarity she was getting. I decided to wait quietly.

At exactly 10:00, an attractive woman with long blonde hair and green eyes opened the door and welcomed me into her room.

"Hello. I'm Tina," she said with a huge smile, extending her hand. "It's so nice to meet you."

"Hi. I'm Susan." We shook hands, and I couldn't help thinking that she looked like Stevie Nicks.

We walked into the room, she gestured to the sofa, and I sat down. She sat across from me and while she was explaining what mediumship is and isn't, I startled hearing the loud click and whoosh of the air conditioning kicking on. I suddenly felt nervous despite her calm demeanor.

*Why did I have to ask so emphatically for Kevin to bring Tripp? What if I offended him by focusing on Tripp? What if Kevin doesn't show up?*

I was kicking myself for not being more considerate of Kevin's feelings. She began with a short prayer to set the intention, asking for divine, uplifting information to help me feel clear and connected and to know everything is alright and in divine order.

"You are welcome to record the reading with your phone," she said, prompting me to fish my iPhone from my pocket. I tapped on the voice memo app and hit record.

"You can put your phone on the coffee table between us so it's closer."

I put my phone down, and right away Tina started with a chuckle "Sorry to laugh, but I heard a fun and excited 'Hi, Mom!'"

I sat with my notebook and pen in hand trying to conceal my feelings of relief. She knew I was here for the HPH conference, which gave her the knowledge I had a child in Spirit, but nevertheless, I was relieved to hear "Hi, Mom."

"Do you know why ..." Tina started but hesitated for a moment and folded her hands shifting to all seriousness. "I know this sounds really wild—and sometimes it can be from the future—but do you know why daisies are important? They are showing me a field of daisies."

My breath caught in my throat while I absorbed what she had just asked.

*I never shared the daisy story on social media or anywhere other than with Tom. There is no way she could know this.*

When I didn't answer, she leaned toward me and continued. "You have a lot of animal energy around you, and you have a child who is showing me daisies as a confirmation of something."

"Oh, wow." I was stunned.

She suddenly started laughing like she was in on a joke. "He's laughing! He's saying you almost miss the dog more than him right now!" and slapped her knee, enjoying Kevin's sense of humor.

I sat frozen in shock, looking at her with my mouth agape.

*She has to be certain of what she is hearing. Under any other circumstances, I might find her comment offensive.* I was staring at her, holding my pen, unable to write this magical exchange down.

*I hope there isn't a glitch in the recording so I can play this back to Tom.*

Tina interpreted my blank expression as being somewhat offended but confidently stood her ground.

She leaned forward again, her tone certain. "He says there is some truth to this statement, and you were hoping an animal would come through today."

I nodded "yes" in agreement.

"Trust me," she said, "This does not happen in every reading!" and she let out another giggle.

My voice finally came to me. "I just had this conversation with him last night." She nodded her head like she heard this all the time.

I could tell she had believed me, so I stopped my explanation. I also didn't want her to lose the connection with Kevin.

She smiled approvingly and said, "You and your son talk all the time. You have an ongoing communication that you are really trusting."

By then, I was smiling with my whole head and paused, putting my hand over my heart, feeling the awe of our connection. Leave it to Kevin to call me out on it, teasing me about my mistake. It was exactly something he'd say if he were standing in front of me.

"He's laughing," Tina said and cupped her hands around her mouth like she was holding a megaphone. "He says he's got the dog!" she said loudly.

My mood had completely shifted from initially being nervous to relaxed as if this was a completely natural and normal conversation. Tina was confirming what I had been feeling all along, and it felt glorious. We were both laughing like old friends, then she suddenly, got quiet again and tilted her head. He was telling her something else.

"Your son is encouraging you to write a book."

I stopped laughing and paused. "How do you feel about that?" she asked.

"I'm not sure," I said honestly.

"He's telling me you've been asking more from him, and you've been getting it."

"Yes, I started journaling my meditations and dreams a couple of years ago in an attempt to connect with him. Our connection has been getting stronger and stronger."

She tilted her head to listen, then leaned forward in her chair toward me.

"He will help you," she said in all seriousness. "You are supposed to write a book. He's saying you're supposed to write down what happened and put it into a book."

•  •  •

Two days later, I was boarding the flight home, still reeling from all I had received, especially the conversation with Tina. I remembered I could only get seat number 27 for the flight to Arizona but not for the return flight home. I walked past the seat and smiled at the passenger sitting in it as I proceeded to mine.

I stowed my carry-on bag in the overhead compartment and took my seat alongside the tiny window, resting my phone and journal on my lap. I had anticipated being nervous for the flight without my 27-safety net, but all I could feel was excitement. I had called Tom as soon as I had finished with Tina, and I was certain he could feel me smiling with my whole head through the airwaves.

I looked out the window onto the tarmac thinking about how far I had come since Kevin's passing. My memories were vivid images imprinted in my mind, yet describing the emotions was where words failed me. I could never seem to capture just how terrifying and isolating the deep pit of grief was with the many ways it took me under, suffocating me. I knew how frustrated I felt to have so much still unexpressed. *What if sharing my experiences sheds light on stigma and the suffering it causes? What if my story could show the healing power of the human-canine connection? What if sharing all the amazing signs and the connection I've had with Kevin could give hope to another parent or anyone in deep grief?* I looked out the window, mulling over my thoughts, watching the airport become smaller and finally disappear.

It was just a few years ago when I was driving home from the National and got the call. I thought about Manny and Tripp and how they took it upon themselves to help me survive in a world that no longer had Kevin in it. My dogs were the ones who could reach me when no one else could. I could have never imagined a few years later that I would spend an uplifting weekend at a conference for parents who had experienced a similar fate. I did not yet know that Kevin and I would find ways to communicate with each other and that he would still be able to make me laugh. I could have never imagined my life having purpose and joy again. But it happened. All of it.

I reached into my purse and pulled out a pen. I opened my journal and skimmed through my conference notes, arriving at a blank page. I slid my hand across the clean sheet of paper and at the top, wrote "TINA READING." I reached in my pocket for my earbuds, plugged the end into my iPhone, and placed the buds into my ears. Leaning back, I settled into my seat and closed my eyes. I could see them all—Kevin in the middle flanked by our Goldens of the past. He was smiling with his whole head. My supporters, my team, *just across the veil.*

I smiled back at them, "I love you, guys."

Ready to take notes, I clicked the top of my pen and hit the play button, beginning the recording.

# How About Yes?

*February 2020–April 2021*

Kevin died six years ago, and there isn't a day that goes by when I don't think of him. In some way, it's a relief to know that there isn't an ending point to grief because if there was, I wouldn't be there. I will always have the scars from outliving my son and feel sorrow over the many micro losses because of it.

When he died, I was desperate for direction on how to live without him in the world. I learned the hard way that there is no winning in grief, no prize for suffering the most or the longest. There are no absolutes or definites or a how-to manual on how to navigate grief, move forward, or live again.

At the beginning of this journey, I remember constantly hearing a phrase I bristled at: "your new normal," which essentially means how you would define your life after loss.

I resented being reminded of what I no longer had. It took countless tears and inward-facing questions, but I have learned to accept this term by defining it as my pain and joy coexisting.

More recently, I was introduced to the term "collateral beauty." Collateral beauty is finding the good that has come from his death, and *that* I can get my head around. Of course, I would trade all of it if I could have him back with me on this earthly plane. But I can't.

For me, the collateral beauty is that I have gotten to know and love myself on a deeper level. I know the power of forgiveness, and that it is a gift I give to myself. I know the healing power of a dog's love. I know that consciousness is limitless, and love never dies. I know by accepting that everything in life is fluid and knowing I have choices on how I respond, the freer I will be from suffering.

I've always strived to be above average, to always be making progress. It took me a very long time to accept that grief is not linear and that it is normal for it to be one step forward and two steps back. Grief itself is fluid; it changes. I can be feeling good for a long time, then suddenly have a hard day, or week, or more. As long as I honor my feelings, there is no cause to panic; I won't stay there. My dogs were the perfect examples of living presently. I've learned through experience that flowing with my pain is not being passive; it is actively inviting grace into my life.

When I think of "choice," I think of Kevin asking me for something he wanted with a "How about yes?" while tapping the tips of his fingers together in anticipation of my answer. One of Kevin's greatest qualities was his open mind. Asking myself "How about yes?" has become my litmus test. Instead of keeping with the status quo or saying *noIcannotpossiblydothat*, I ask myself "How about yes?" and decide based on how it feels in my gut.

Going through life this way has forced me to continuously question everything: my beliefs, my values, and what I invite into my life. It has forced me to look deep within myself to find what is true and right for me. Thankfully, I've said yes to my sense of humor and enjoy laughing when it comes. When I *think* my way to any decision, I always check in with my heart to test if it still holds true. This is how I live with what I cannot fix and also how I live by what serves and brings me joy.

In February of 2020, as the pandemic was hitting the globe, we had to euthanize Manny. He had been diagnosed with lymphoma a few months prior to making it to twelve and a half years old before he let us know it was time. He had continued his volunteer work right up to the end as an attentive listener and friend. He was adored by all the children he served at the library, in grief groups, or by being part of a team of dogs who participated in fundraisers for the local hospice organization. Manny was now with Tripp and Kevin, supporting me from across the veil.

I had been putting the word out into the golden retriever community that I was looking for a new puppy, and after careful consideration, I chose a male puppy from a litter that was born on February 7, 2020 and named him Rune. It wasn't until I wrote out his birthdate as 2/7 that I specifically knew Kevin had been involved with the selection.

By the time Rune came home with me, it was April of 2020. The pandemic had forced us into lockdowns, and there weren't any puppy classes for puppy parents to attend. During the pandemic, there was also a huge influx of people wanting puppies since everyone was stuck at home.

I knew how important socializing and training were during a puppy's first year and the potential behavior issues they would be facing in a few months because of our global circumstances. I finally saw a way to make an impact with what I loved to do, which was how to properly raise a puppy and create a human-canine bond that would last a lifetime.

When Rune was eight weeks old, I began documenting the socializing and training I was doing with him. I made videos with my phone and wrote out detailed instructions and explanations for what I was doing in each daily post. I logged Rune's first twelve months of training in a Facebook group called Life with Rune, archiving the lessons so future puppy parents could start from the beginning.

In a little over a year, it was a community that grew organically to 2,000+ members. I developed my website and started building an email list—I just kept taking the next best step I could, not always recognizing what I was creating but knowing I was heading in the right direction. I was truly being led every step of the way.

And, in 2021, I was awarded the Rachel Page Elliot Lifetime Achievement Award from the Golden Retriever Club of America for my dedication to educating people on how to train their puppies in the Life with Rune Facebook group. It was an achievement I never would have imagined a few years ago but one that has filled me to the brim because even after I stopped competing, the GRCA has been a home away from home. They're my people, and dogs are my world. Receiving this honor was like a homecoming except in a new season of my life. In this season, I'm not serving for the purpose of recognition and ribbons and trophies but serving to have meaning in my life.

Life with Rune came to me as an idea to serve in a way that felt good to me. The idea to help others was sparked by giving a homeless man a bowl of soup, and Life with Rune became the polished version of that intention. It was me in my lane, serving in a way that was aligned with my skills and passions. And with every step I've taken, I've asked, "How about yes?" and have kept moving if that next step has resounded in my heart fully.

Life with Rune didn't only serve others, it served me in ways I couldn't predict. It gave me the confidence to push myself further into things I had never done but felt called to do, such as write this book.

When I first began thinking about the book, an ad for an online course called Writing Through Grief and Trauma arrived in my email inbox. It was the perfect sign to get going. I signed up for the class and after the introduction, we were given fifteen minutes to write about our feelings uncensored. The writing prompt was "How do you feel when you tell your story?" The first sentence I wrote, ironically, was "I don't have a story." But I kept going, and I kept writing; and after the fifteen minutes were up, I read what I had written.

I had poured my heart out over the sadness and anger of not knowing what happened the night Kevin died. Here I was, years later, still holding onto some resentment. Right then, I knew I had a choice. And perhaps in telling my story, I could finally rewrite the narrative. I wanted to see the story of Kevin, not the story of his death.

In making the decision to write this book, I began to see the positive impact my story could have for someone else. Writing my story wouldn't just be healing for me but could also be healing for others. A big part of my goal in writing this book is to shine a light on stigma by humanizing overdose and how it affects the people who loved them. If we think in terms of "good" and "bad" ways to die, we are inadvertently measuring the value of the person's life.

Kevin was a son, a brother, a grandson, a cousin, and a friend. He loved his family, friends, music, and the outdoors. He was kind, sensitive, friendly, funny, and creative. Kevin isn't defined by the cause of his death; he's defined by the way he lived his life. I want others who have experienced a similar loss to see that making peace with the circumstances surrounding their loved one's death can help them remember more of who they were as a person.

As this book got closer to its completion, I knew I wanted to launch it on the day Kevin passed (October 3rd), associating something positive with that day. I wanted to honor the collateral beauty from this loss as well as the life he lived and symbolically give voice and recognition to all the parents who had lost a child too soon, no matter the reason. Of course, Kevin would give me his opinion on this idea. After some research online, I learned that every October 3rd is National Kevin Day. I could just picture him laughing at the clever way he chose to let me know he was happy about it!

I think one of the most incredible gifts is that no matter how long Life with Rune lasts or how big it grows and no matter what comes of this book landing in the hands of the people who need it, I know Kevin is always with me. I can't stress that enough. Now that my mind and heart are open to receiving signs from him, I know he's always close by.

He is good at balancing the obvious signs (like Kevin the dog and National Kevin Day) with the more subtle ones. The obvious ones are so remarkable they get a full-on belly laugh, and I think of the subtle ones as his way to remind me to keep trusting that he is always with me. The subtle signs are the ordinary things that happen the moment I'm thinking about him—a special song that comes on the radio or the light that flickers. Sometimes I even hear his laugh when

I laugh. These are all just as important (and more frequent) as the bigger ones.

I suppose if anything I would want you to take away from my experience in hopes it may help you on your own path it would be this:

Grief is always a work in progress. On a practical level, if you are grieving over a loved one (human or pet), I would invite you to take time to sit alone with your pain. After you've shed an ocean of tears, inch your way forward by noticing what gives you even the tiniest lift. Is it taking a walk in nature? Is it watching the birds at your bird feeder or at a park? Is it volunteering in some capacity, even if it's just once per month? Whatever it is, make it a priority by doing it often.

Then look at parts of your old life that are a burden or that make you feel worse. Are there ways you can modify or eliminate them? Knowing the what's and why's of your feelings highlights where you can adjust. Even a small adjustment can be empowering during a time when you feel that nothing is in your control. This is what I refer to as *trying on your old life to see what still fits.* Maybe something just needs to be put aside for a while, and you return to it at a later time. On a spiritual level, don't dismiss the signs your loved one is sending! Thank them for their efforts to connect with you. Talk to them; they are listening. Join a support group to meet people who share in the kind of loss you've experienced. There can be comfort in just being with people who understand your loss and knowing you are not alone.

Thanks to Kevin, Manny, Tripp, and what they've taught me, I have solid emotional ground beneath me. As I knew he would, my new puppy, Rune, has been working his magic with my heart since he arrived. We are thoroughly enjoying each other's companionship, and I love that he plays a role in helping me empower puppy parents in the Life with Rune Facebook group.

Someday we will all be together again, but until then, I honor them by living a life they would want for me. I ask myself "How about yes?" often as a reminder to stay open to a life that has hope, purpose, joy, and laughter. Just a few years ago, I asked if my life was just going to be something to endure. I am so grateful to have finally found my answer.

# Reader Questions

Dear Reader,

I wrote this book with the hope that it would help open the discussion of two topics that are not discussed enough in grief—the effects of stigma over how a person dies and how comfort can often be found in what we cannot explain with logic. Signs from loved ones across the veil give us hope and the feeling we are still connected to them, two things we seek when we are grieving.

I also wanted to pay homage to the role our dogs play in supporting us through healing and trauma and, generally, how they have the ability to make us better human beings. Perhaps you've felt this way at various times in your life with your own dogs.

In the event you want to dive deeper with this book, I've developed these questions for you to use as a guide. My hope is that in reflecting on these questions, you gain some insight into your own experience with grief, stigma, signs, and/or the relationship you have with the dog(s) in your life.

You may choose to contemplate these privately, with a friend, or in a book club discussion.

Wishing you peace on your journey.

With love,

Susan

1. Did Susan's experiences with stigma surprise you? In thinking about some of the situations she experienced, which stood out, and what was it about that moment that made it memorable or relevant to you?

2. Have you experienced stigma over how someone close to you died? If so, what was your experience, and how did it affect you? What did you find helpful in coping with the stigma?

3. Although not a lot of time is spent discussing the differences in how they grieve, it is clear Susan finds some comfort being around other parents who have lost a child in support groups, but Tom never attends support groups; and Matthew doesn't want to discuss his grief. Have you ever experienced grief differently than someone you live with? Did you think they weren't doing it "right" because they did it differently from you? How did you manage the differences in your grief styles?

4. Manny and Tripp took on the role of supporting Susan right away. What do you think they did best to support Susan in the way she needed it most? Have you ever had a dog support you during a hard time in your life? If so, what did you learn from them? How is their support different from support from family and friends?

5. Did Susan's experience give you a better understanding of what stigma does to the family and friends who are

grieving loved ones who overdose? Did her story validate your own feelings in any way? What part(s) of her story specifically resonated with you? Please describe.

6. The day after Kevin's services, Susan and Tom got their first sign from Kevin. What do you think Kevin the dog gave Susan so early in her grief journey? If you've received signs from a loved one who has passed, what was the first sign you remember receiving, and how did it make you feel?

7. A big part of Susan's healing is spent sitting alone in Kevin's room with the pain and in meditation. How do you think this daily practice helped her? When you've grieved, have you had any process or ritual that has brought you comfort or enlightenment?

8. Susan has a lucid dream visit from Kevin where he tells her that his messages will have the number 27. One bowl of soup happens on the 27th of the month, and Rune was born on 2/7. Do you and your deceased loved one have a special number or sign between you to say hello or to send messages?

9. In Chapter 12, the idea for Susan to meet Kevin on the horizon came from the poem "Gone From My Sight" by Henry Van Dyke. Initially, Susan is excited when she sees the dot in the photo, but when she figures it's a lens flare and not an orb, her excitement wanes. Have you ever talked yourself out of a sign you felt was from your loved one? What does it feel like in your body when you KNOW you've received a sign?

10. Grief can bring up old wounds that we've not dealt with. Susan was afraid of how angry she felt when she was told by the reporter that her story would not be published without including the cause of death. Society has conditioned us to believe that anger is a

"bad" emotion, but anger can be motivating and useful in grief and worth exploring where it originates. Have you ever explored your anger in grief to see where it leads? If so, were you able to find the root of it? What other emotions came up during grief that you found useful? What came from feeling them and exploring them?

# Acknowledgments

I am lucky to have been blessed with some extraordinary people and dogs whom I'd like to acknowledge here.

My dearest Kevin, you are my North Star. Thank you for shining so brightly that I could find you when I was lost and for always showing up in a way that I can understand.

Tom, you are my soulmate, my best friend who walks this path with me. Thank you for listening, supporting, and believing in me. But, most especially, thank you for making me laugh so hard it feels like exercise. You are my most treasured yes. I love you.

Matthew, thank you for writing some of the most beautiful words I've ever read. My eternal wish is that you always know how much I love you.

Manny and Tripp, you were the ones who could reach me when no one else could. You were my loving caretakers, my guardian angels in fur coats. Thank you for your patience, loyalty, and devotion.

Thank you to my family, Weezie, JD, Kathy, Larry, Michael, Lynne, brothers-in-law, sisters-in-law, and the cousins for your love and support. I cherish the time we spend together now and from before October 3, 2015—especially the ones at Lake Winnipesaukee and Costa Rica.

Kelsey, to say "thank you" seems so inadequate. During a time when he needed it most, you were there for him. Thank you from the bottom of my heart.

Thank you to my friends and mentors: Bliss, Rick, Celeste, Kathy, Milly, Donna, and Jan. We met through dogs and became friends, and you each have impacted my life tremendously. I am so grateful for your friendship, the laughs, and all I've learned from you.

Thank you to Amy, Michelle, Michele, and Nancy—my forever girls of more than forty years and still going strong.

Thank you, Debbie, for giving me the right book at the right time, the lasagna, the sausage bread, and all the laughter. Who knew a chip falling from the sky could be so funny?

Thank you to Kevin's friends who wrote the most loving tributes on his Facebook wall. You will never know what your words meant to me.

A special thank you to Ally, my writing coach. Ally, you have given me the tools to get what was in my heart onto paper, helping me honor Kevin and my journey in a way that I am so proud of. Thank you from the bottom of my heart—YOU ROCK!

Thank you, Tanya. It was no coincidence that I had established myself as a client with you several months before Kevin passed. Thank you for all your expertise and care in approaching my physical and emotional health as a whole.

Thank you, Kim. Meeting and working with you gave me clarity on what I came to do in this life and gave me the validation I needed.

*Acknowledgments*

Thank you to my publisher, Bridgett McGowen-Hawkins, founder of BMcTALKS Press, and her team for all their help getting this book into the world.

Thank you to my first readers Tom, Pat, Paula, Anne, and Rob who read the early draft of my manuscript. I am so grateful for the generosity of your time and detailed feedback, helping make this book the best version of itself.

Thank you, Jonathan C. Chase, for your dedication to the golden retriever breed and your wonderful endorsement.

Thank you, spiritual medium, Tina Powers, for relaying the daisies, for giving me the idea to write this book, and for your beautiful endorsement.

Thank you to Helping Parents Heal for providing resources to parents, being Shining Lights for others, and letting them know that healing is possible. My sincere gratitude especially to Elizabeth Boisson, Irene Vouvalides, Carol Allen, and Lynn Hollahan for reading the final draft and providing endorsements.

Thank you to Sabrina, Deb, Marta, Amy, Gail, and Katie for reading my last draft and sharing your thoughts and reviews, which I've happily added to the front of this book.

Thank you to The Compassionate Friends for the practical advice, support, and for witnessing my grief.

Thank you to spiritual medium Necole Stephens who gave me a hello from across the veil with the words "A small, thin piece of paper in the tall dresser." That proof sent me on a path to learn how to connect with Kevin on my own.

Many thanks to my friends in the Golden Retriever Club of America and Yankee Golden Retriever Club for their continued dedication to dog sports and our shared passion for the golden retriever.

Thank you, David Kessler, for the work you've done and continue to do to help those grieving. Even your voice is a balm for an aching heart.

Thank you, Tom Zuba, for writing *Permission to Mourn: A New Way to Do Grief*, specifically the chapters "Choosing to Heal" and "Question Everything."

Thank you, Brené Brown, for all your work to educate people on the effects of shame and the power of vulnerability.

Thank you, Paul Simon, for connecting generations with your music. A couple years after Kevin died, I looked up the inspiration for the song "Mother and Child Reunion" as I very much wanted it to be symbolic of Kevin and me. I laughed out loud when I read the title idea came from a chicken and egg dish from a Chinese restaurant menu. Of course, I knew Kevin was laughing when I told him, which only solidified it as our song.

Thank you, Rune, for working your magic on my heart, carrying the torch from the dogs who came before you.

Thank you to those who offer comfort and support with their therapy animals. Your time and effort make the world a better place.

Lastly, I'd like to thank you, the reader. As I wrote this book, I've kept you in mind with the sincere hope that you find peace along your own journey by walking along with me on mine.

# About the Author

Susan Lynch has trained and competed with her golden retrievers for more than twenty years and has been an active member of the Golden Retriever Club of America (GRCA) and Yankee Golden Retriever Club (YGRC) since 1995. She previously sat on the Yankee Golden Retriever Club Board of Directors from 2008 to 2016 in the roles of director, vice president, and president. Her knowledge base covers both competitive and non-competitive American Kennel Club sports that include hunt tests, field trials, obedience trials, and conformation shows. Additionally, four of her dogs were active, certified therapy dogs with Therapy Dogs International.

In 2021, Susan was awarded the Rachel Page Elliott Featherquest Lifetime Achievement Award from the GRCA for her contributions to puppy education through Life with Rune, a Facebook group and community she founded. In Life with Rune, Susan demonstrates puppy socializing and training techniques that are critical from eight weeks through twelve months. Susan is on a mission to use her own vast experience and expertise in dog training and her personal journey through loss to support families in grief by showing them the power and depth of canine companionship during trauma.

If you would like to know more about Susan and her work inside Life with Rune, you can visit her website, susanlynch.com. This is also where you can contact her for speaking engagements and find a collection of photos from the stories depicted in this book. To hear from Susan regularly, sign up for her email list, also found on her website. Most importantly, if you loved this book and would recommend it to a friend, please write and share a review where you've purchased the book and share it with Susan via the contact form on her website.

CPSIA information can be obtained
at www.ICGtesting.com
Printed in the USA
BVHW042341250922
647977BV00005B/145

9 781953 315212